MUELOS

A Stone Age Superstition About Sexuality

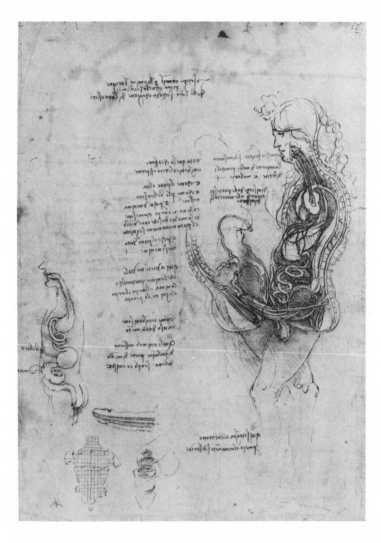

Leonardo da Vinci, sagittal section drawing.

Quaderni d'Anatomia, 19097v, III, 3v. Royal Library, Windsor Castle. By gracious permission of H. M. Queen Elizabeth II.

MUELOS

A Stone Age Superstition
About Sexuality

Weston La Barre

COLUMBIA UNIVERSITY PRESS
NEW YORK   1984

Library of Congress Cataloging in Publication Data

La Barre, Weston, 1911–
   Muelos : A Stone Age superstition about sexuality.
   1. Sex customs–History.   2. Marrow–Folklore.
3. Semen–Folklore.   4. Head-hunters.   5. Hunting
customs–History.   I. Title.
GN484.3.L3 1984   392   84-14232
ISBN 0-231-05960-4 (alk. paper)
ISBN 0-231-05961-2 (pbk. : alk. paper)

Columbia University Press
New York   Guilford, Surrey
Copyright © 1985 Columbia University Press
All rights reserved

Printed in the United States of America

Clothbound editions of Columbia University Press Books are
Smyth-sewn and printed on permanent and durable acid-free paper.

Designed by Ken Venezio

For Steven Kane

Contents

Preface

The supposition that we might know, even fragmentarily, something that went on in the minds of Old Stone Age men is on the face of it extravagant and hardly believable. Yet we securely know (from mere linguistic cues in living speech) the name, pronunciation, and attributes of the supreme god *diew*,[1] together with a detailed body of data about Indo-European culture reaching back to the pre−Bronze Age chalcolithic period, several millennia before the art of writing reached their north European homeland. Again, who would have thought that measuring carbon$_{14}$ content would give us something like an absolute date for the weaving of a grass sandal found in the ruins of a prehistoric pueblo? By measuring the isotopes of oxygen, the atomic physicist H. C. Urey knew that a Jurassic fossil belemnite, roughly 150 million years old, began life in the spring, lived in a summer water temperature of 68°−70° F. (59°−64° F. in winter), and died four years later. And with glottochronological linguistic techniques and a study of native marriage customs, Gajdusek tested whether the puzzling degenerative central nervous system disease *kuru* of the montane New Guinea Fore tribe might be genetic.

In the light of these discoveries, the necessary assumption of the scientist must be that anything that ever happens in the universe may leave some traces and thus can be potentially recoverable. All that is needed is familiarity with the data and understanding of the method of observing them—for scientific insight results to an amazing degree simply from a new way of looking at data accessible to anyone. In the present case, a somewhat old-fashioned training in descriptive world ethnography provided the comparative information; and the flagrant wrongness of the superstition, both anatomically and physiologically, made it stand out for examination in each of its repeated appearances — until, after some decades of my exposure to it, folkloristic fact and the manifest theory behind it have emerged and merged. An erroneous belief about sexuality has survived some hundreds of centuries.

Objectively unrelated specific elements, found again and again in arbitrary combination in the belief complex, inescapably show common origin. The intercontinental distribution of the concept argues great antiquity. That the notion revealed is quite wholly erroneous indicates that it could not have been learned repeatedly from the book of nature. To state that observed similarities constitute a mystical "archetype" merely names the phenomenon and hints mysteriously at its ubiquity, doing nothing to explain its origin, rationale, or validity. In the end, the simplest explanation is that the widely diffused, though wrong, notion is a very old element in an ancient paleolithic *Ur-Kultur*, descended in its variants into widely varied contexts — hunting rites, initiation ceremonies, European-Asiatic and New World headhunting, Hindu religion, European literature, and classical Platonic metaphysics — but still unmistakably recognizable for its bizarre, stubborn, complex quiddity.

Some important implications for culture follow. The antiquity of a belief can give no assurance of its tested truth. To depend here for belief not only betrays the infantile behavior of the authoritarian personality but also supposes, outrageously, that men have learned nothing since their remotest ancestors. Such cowardly fundamentalism abdicates responsibility for our own reality testing. The criterion for truth of an idea is not its longevity. Nor is it even a majority *consensus gentium* vote of mankind. The wisdom of the ages may be only the entrenched ignorance of frightened primitive minds.

There is no kind of evolutionary "natural selection" among ideas. There is only the continued steadfastness of nature as touchstone for validity, which we must have the courage and the wit to consult.

A second falsehood concerning culture is that survival of a belief firmly attests to its continuing functionality. Now, it is easy to see how a belief could in origin serve a clear function — such as the belief in immortality as a defense against the narcissistically unfaceable fact of death. It is also easy to see how such a motivated superstition might continue to have the same function indefinitely. But to argue, as does Marvin Harris, that *every* long-surviving belief has its (probably Marxian) function *now* is to take on an interminable task of jesuitic rationalization. Indeed, a Boasian–Benedictine egalitarianism requires extension of the functionalist franchise to all cultures — hence we find Harris arguing that the Hindu totemic taboo on cow-killing gives a huge reservoir of protein to Untouchables.[2]

There is a third contemporary talmudism regarding culture, that of the French structuralists, who suppose that rational structure (albeit unknown to the believers) always lurks hidden beneath the surface of any cognitive system whatever. A Bororo belief must have some kind of structure we can rationalize. It depends only on our civilized cleverness. It is difficult to avoid the perception that the ethnological hermeneutics of Lévi-Strauss is the latest deism. It would find the ineluctable, somewhat despairingly and cynically to be sure, in the very ways the cogs of the human brain grind together—a fairly useless epistemology even if true.

What the theologians of ethnology will not countenance is that beliefs, even of groups, may be as fully awry as those of a psychotic individual. There is a hidden yearning that Culture *ipso facto* might provide some discoverable grain of truth — and surely the mass of mankind must somehow be reliably right? On the contrary, culture is commonly only another defense mechanism: it can not provide a technique for finding truth. We are once again reduced to the epistemological humility of the scientist, eternally tentative in his beliefs but nevertheless endlessly hopeful in offering up his cognitive myths to the arbitrament of nature, struggling to be aware of the contribution to myth in his very hypothesis, and ruefully acknowledging that although thinking contaminates perception, perception is impossible without thought.

A major difficulty in "popularizing" psychiatry, or even in imparting its discoveries to well-disposed and quite sane individuals, is that the minds of psychotics are full of nightmarish fantasies and preoccupations repugnant to properly repressed normal persons. In the anxiety aroused by such spectacles as a psychotic mind, a common defense is to argue that the discoveries of doctors are their own inventions. The argument is not without merit that the practice of psychiatry should be confined to physicians, because only they have been exposed in their training to the blood and guts of the human animal, and are emotionally prepared to face the ugliness of illness.

If, even in metaphor, we may contend that the sickness of societies rests in their forgotten history, then the anthropologist must expect to encounter the same repugnant gruesomeness in his study of men in groups. Since all thinking men now face the same terror — the extinction of our species — they may grudgingly attend to such a thesis as that wars depend to an alarming degree on the treacherous holy fantasy (false but insatiably desired) of individual immortality, and on each man's denied oedipal murderousness. But what are we to say to the discovery of cultural madnesses that implicate manhood itself with headhunting, scalping, perverse sexual practices, and the morass of hallucinogenic drugs? For the reason that direct evidence is better than secondary interpretation, I have been generous with direct quotation of authorities. And because the determined student may wish to examine sources for himself, a harvest of these is supplied. But perhaps the reader should not anticipate bland gentilities behind any madness of mankind.

I wish to express appreciation of the Rockefeller Foundation for my appointment as a Visiting Scholar at the Villa Serbelloni, at

Bellagio on Lake Como, where I began this book. Because of the temerity of its thesis, the reader will condone the meticulous, even burdensome, documentation which seemed necessary for firsthand reference on seemingly diverse subjects.

Notes

1. The usual derivation of *diew* is "the shining one" (Aust, Thulin) or "bright" (Max Müller, *Science of Language,* 2d series, p. 473). But Grace Sturtevant Hopkins ("Indo-European *deiwos* and Related Words," *Language Dissertations,* 1932, no. 12, p. 45) argues for "sky" — a term which does not encompass the actual metaphorical forms of deity in Indo-European usage any more than do specific sun, moon, planets, fire, light, etc. that earlier etymologists endlessly argued over. Each polemicist was right that his favorite detected metaphor must be included as a sometime meaning, but only the generic abstraction satisfactorily fits them all. Buck believes Hopkins has a "needless doubt of the underlying notion of 'bright'" — which consensus Buck endorses. Carl D. Buck, *A Dictionary of Selected Synonyms in the Principal Indo-European Languages: A Contribution to the History of Ideas* (Chicago: University of Chicago Press, 1949), p. 1464.

2. Marvin Harris, "The Cultural Ecology of India's Sacred Cattle," *Current Anthropology,* 1966, 7:51 – 59; Harris, *Cows, Pigs, Wars, and Witches: The Riddle of Culture* (New York: Random House, 1974), pp. 11 – 12. That some superstitions are beneficial is an old theme from James G. Frazer's *Psyche's Task* (London: Macmillan, 1913). In one of Harris' colleagues the theme degenerates into jesuitic rationalizing of "some good" in even the most noxious practices, e.g., that incessant headhunting "was relief from boredom" and unified (to what end, better headhunting?) the unrelated husbands in a society with matrilocal marriage.

MUELOS
A Stone Age Superstition About Sexuality

All known cultures derive eventually from a generalized Paleolithic culture.

Clyde Kluckhohn

It will, I think, appear that the fundamental beliefs traceable in the language and the earliest literature of Greece and Rome...were, in some cases at least, already current in the Old Stone Age, explaining curious practices then; and live on unrecognized in customs and idioms of today.

Richard Onians

Introduction

The oldest ritual of which we have any knowledge is the rite at the site of the ancient hunter's kill. The rite is partly propitiation of the animal's spirit for stealing its life to feed one's own and is partly expression of a concern that animals be available again in the future. Life in animals and men is enough alike to assimilate the animal's feelings to one's own, and the ritual is essentially both placation and a magical undoing. In order for the animal to come to life again, the hunter puts the bones, often only the head and the feet, in proper anatomical position — and the animal, reconstituted and clothed in flesh, will return alive.

The first mystery is death, and it permeates all later religion. The hunter is the eater of life, that mysterious and dramatic difference between the living body and the dead. The skull and bones (as we shall see), or more properly the head and the skeleton, are regarded as the germinal source of animal life, and capable of reproducing the whole. The immense antiquity of the rite is shown in its near universality among hunting peoples; indeed, it can be inferred that the bone cult was an original part of the Old Stone Age *Ur-Kultur*.[1] American and European prehistorians consider that such ritual-induced immortality of animals is an even older belief than that of human immortality, which is based on it. The bone cult is even older than the ubiquitous "master of animals," which is a kind of anthropomorphic personalizing of this species-generative force.[2] Motivation to belief in both animal and human immortality is plain enough, for the fact of death is manifest in each hunt — of the animal slain, it is to be hoped, but sometimes death of the hunter instead. It is life that is the assumed normal state, whereas birth and death are the mysteries to be explained.

The material world can be taken for granted. It just always is. Change is the puzzle. Life comes and goes, a mysterious X, the algebraic difference between a live body and a dead one. Manifestly, it has to do with breath or warmth (or, quintessentially, fire, light). The *anima* that "animates," though ever unseen, is the soul or spirit, more permanent as pattern, certainly, than any individual animal is.

Animistic belief in a separable soul, besides explaining life and death, serves also to explain the mysterious persistent *patterning* in animals, since no matter how many individual animals are killed by hunters, and their flesh eaten by the people, the animal species remains abundant, in a kind of immortal *logos*-pattern that remains unchanged — a mysterious principle, evidently male, inherent in bones, the fundamental framework of life. For it can easily be observed that only through the intervention of a male principle is reproduction possible, the supposed stamping of pattern upon formless materia-substance. The growth of a child in a woman's body is no mystery. The increment comes from the food the mother eats, quite as later growth comes from the milk she gives her child. The mystery lies in the inception of life: consciousness, life, warmth appear to be a male gift, and surely from his semen. The elaboration of this age-old confusion between *consciousness* and *life* forms the substance of the present study.

Since semen is the material vehicle of life, the question becomes the origin of semen. It is here that consciousness and life become inextricably melded. The head is easily ascertained to be the main site of the senses. Closing the lids extinguishes eyesight, and turning the head alters the field of vision, as does darkness (hence light is a critical component of life consciousness). Hands over the ears muffle hearing. Taste seems to be in the mouth, smell in the nose. Of course the matter is not so simple, for the sense of touch is widely dispersed in the body, like heat-, pain-, and cold-awareness, proprioceptive kinesthesia, etc. And life surely remains related to breath and warmth, all of which complications account for many alternatives to the head as seat-of-the-soul familiar to anthropologists. However, we are concerned here only with the head as the traditional site of consciousness and hence life.

If bones are the framework of life, more specifically it is the semen-like marrow *(muelos)* in the bones that is believed to be the source of semen. The skull, as the bone enclosing the most plentiful *muelos*-marrow in the body (the brain), is therefore the major repository of the generative life-stuff or semen. Consciousness and life are the same stuff and thus have the same site. The idea seems bizarre and contrived to us only because we have forgotten the formative origins of our ideas. Yet, as later discussion will establish, the concept of brain-*muelos* as the source of semen is everywhere inherent in European thinking, as well as in that of societies elsewhere.

That the goddess Athena should spring directly from the brain-*muelos* of her sire Zeus, parthenogenetically as it were, would seem perfectly plausible to a classic Greek (as simply as Aphrodite could arise in the sea-foam from Ouranos). Given the same notion of brain-*muelos*, Shakespeare could have Parolles accuse Bertram of "spending his manly marrow in her arms" *(All's Well That Ends Well,* II, iii, 284).

That a literary man should perpetuate ancient errors is understandable enough. More difficult to comprehend is that so observant an anatomist as Leonardo da Vinci should persist in the error of supposing a connection of semen and brain. Leonardo made a full dozen of coition studies in his anatomical drawings, yet in at least one sagittal section of the male he shows ducts to convey the brain-*muelos* from the cerebrospinal canal to the male genital that are in fact not there.

Since other more scientific views of sexuality have tended to displace this ancient nonsense, we have the same disposition to disbelieve that sane men could have believed it, just as we cannot believe a neurotic believes the antic nonsense the psychiatrist discovers him believing. Our right thinking is destructive of conceptual imagination of alternatives. But superstition about the manly marrow is implicit in the Hindu and Christian rationale of "continence" — which aims literally to retain the soul-stuff of life, hence attain immortality, through non-expenditure of it in sexual orgasm. Purity gives permanence, so to speak, and orgastic "sin" is literal death ("every orgasm is a little death"). And psychiatrists still report that adolescent boys fear losing the mind from "loss of manhood," believing that insanity inevitably awaits those who expend the life-stuff through "self-abuse." Again, widespread headhunting, both primitive and ancient European, had as its motive the collection of male strength and fertility (hence no youth could marry before collecting an enemy head, lest the total tribal supply of fertility be depleted).

The concept of *muelos* is therefore not a trivial one, but has fundamental impact on religion, philosophy, sexuality, and war, for all that we have largely forgotten its origins and meaning. The thesis here is not that some mystical Jungian "archetype" is at work, but rather that *muelos* is a cultural belief so very ancient as to have been part of the Paleolithic *Ur-Kultur* postulated by Kluckhohn.[3] There has been subsequently a straightforward cultural transmission of a concept from ancient ethnoanatomy and ethnophysiology for some millennia.

The phenomenon gives rise to several questions: the perseveration of culture even when its origins and rationale are forgotten, and the immortality of error, as well as the curious impotence of scientific discovery to supplant old beliefs. The ascertainable fact is that orgasm has nothing whatever to do with brain-substance, whether its increase or diminution. Likewise, the masculinizing effect of hormones produced by the interstitial Leydig cells of the testis is *wholly separate histologically* from the production of spermatozoa in semen,[4] at the maturation-division of germ-cells proper in testicular spermatocytes. Only removal of the testes by castration will have effect on either type of cell, whether semen- or male hormone-producing. The two types of testicular cells are completely distinct and separate. Further, it has been experimentally proven that the seminiferous tubules are not in any way androgenogenic and, for that matter, by far the major volume of semen is produced elsewhere, in the prostate. Thus whatever happens to semen, legitimately or illegitimately ejaculated, will have no effect on the continued production of male hormones, or their masculinizing potency, or the general I.Q. of the subject. Ejaculation of semen in any guise, therefore, can not be a "loss of manhood" but only an evidence of it. Nor can longevity of the individual be affected in any fashion by this physiological act. Nevertheless, the *muelos*-superstition about sexuality — for superstition it is — can be reliably traced from the Old Stone Age to contemporary times. The theme is the insidious and massive perdurability of culture, even when it is demonstrably mistaken. The method is in part historical— archeological, in part comparative – ethnological, and in part linguistic, modeled on Onians' admirable paleophilological study of *The Origins of European Thought*.

Time, in which all events occur, is the major mystery in the universe — and most especially as time encounters organic systems. We have learned from Freud to see how the neurotic is victim to his forgotten life history. That those who do not understand their history are condemned to be its victims is a principle applicable not only to individuals but also to cultural groups. We need a phylo-analysis of culture as well as the psycho-analysis of individuals in order to liberate ourselves from the past, insofar as either is at all possible. Elsewhere I have shown that each Ghost Dance responding to unresolved cultural problems becomes one of the historic group-neuroses we call religions; in the present study we shall see how antique concepts, unexamined or forgotten, distort secular thinking as well.

One kind of encounter of organisms with time and changing situations is biological evolution. Problems are somehow solved; but each resolution of a problem becomes incorporated into organic structure, and there is limited potential to adapt anew with the same now-committed structure (indeed, all organic life on earth now seems to be inexorably committed to right-handed chemical compounds). True, a rayed fish-fin can become one of four amphibian legs; an amphibian forelimb can become a whale-flipper, a bat-wing, a bird-wing, a mammalian paw, or a hand. In fact, a flightless penguin wing can be recycled into a functional swimming-fin. But we see few enough whale-flippers turning into bat-wings or vice versa, or bird-wings into hands. In a wry sense, "anatomy is destiny" — especially since environmental change, which called forth the major new adaptation, commonly produces secondary adaptations. For example, whale *size*, for which aquatic habitat was the enabling factor, is poorly adaptive for aerial flight.

Further, the amphibian four-limbed plan is a *commitment:* an organism can only adapt with what it has, and given only four fish-fin limbs, all descendants of amphibians—whether birds, bats, apes or porpoises — are inexorably committed to four limbs (or fewer: snakes, as to limbs; penguins and ratite birds, as to functional flying wings). It is genetically so. But did four limbs have to be so "in the nature of things?" Not necessarily. There are also six-legged insects, eight-legged crabs and scorpions, and many-legged centipedes. The poverty of imagination in science-fiction improvisation! The wildest popular imagining of "the man from Mars" (an unlikely planet to begin with) gives us only a green android with two insect antennae — when already, in the real biological world on this earth, fish taste with their skin, some insects hear with their legs, and smell with antennae, and spiders have eight eyes.

The same principle of commitment seems to occur as well in cultural forms, although here seemingly far more arbitrarily than in organic evolution. Discerning that the senses are, in humans, significantly in the head seems to be inevitable *discovery* of a real situation; but just how inevitably did the actual "facts of life" require saddling subsequent mankind with the fallacy that semen is brainstuff? The best we can do is to attempt tracing the lost rationale of false ideas, but here re-examined reality gives us little support or assistance. And since the cultural situation is not confined by any kind of cosmic fact, we could well be wrong in understanding the supposed rationale also, which exists only in human history. It is as though *what got there first* ideologically were important, not whether the notion is accurate. Brain – semen answered a question. It takes a rarer wit to question our answers. Yet so absurd are these antique beliefs that much of our effort here must actually be spent in demonstrating that modern as well as primitive men do in fact hold these beliefs, and without necessarily knowing their origins — and even risk their lives to act upon them. The corollaries of falsehood are horrendous. The origins are gruesome enough; however, headhunting rationale can be more easily accepted, since it is believed by alien savage minds. But is our own sacred belief in individual immortality one root of war, a cultural illness that now threatens the death of our species?

Even more in human history than in organic evolution we can ask "what if?" at every fork in the road. For example, occidental music is based on the outrageously arbitrary dodecatonic scale, which for all the mathematical efforts of Pythagoras quickly becomes totally irrational. One may listen earnestly enough to Bartok and Hindemith, yet the accustomed heart remains in thrall to Haydn and fixated on Mozart. Again, in visual art of the great tradition, every style shows clear revolt from some predecessor in painting or sculpture, each no more arbitrary than the new. The Belvedere torso, that most magnificent chunk of rock on this earth, deeply affected sculptors. But what if it had never been dug up in the Renaissance?

Political conservatism, or reactionism, can explain much concerning Plato, as we shall see — though it is hard to understand even so how our most influential philosopher could have managed to be consistently wrong on every major question, whether in physics, politics, or aesthetics. But did the Great Tradition in western philosophy need to have come in direct lineage from the Old Stone Age master of animals, the Idea as seminal father of all descendant Particulars? Why should the ideological consequence of the Bone Cult of paleolithic hunters still torment Victorian adolescents? Must fantasy usurp for millennia the psychic space that cool information should come to occupy?

The tyrannical perseveration of Pattern! Even in its mutations: the sins of the fathers still hounded Hawthorne. Psychic time is timeless time. Even minutely, in the individual life history, there is the element of historical contingency. In the human, each historical happenstance turns *experience* into the *structure* of personality—in increasing antiquity and hence permanence successively: for example, in one life, a circus and sudden storm in 1915 that loosened great tentpoles to fall on dangerous-animal enclosures; echoes of the eighteenth-century burning at the stake of a youth of eighteen in the memory of a family; and even more since still earlier the fate of that man who was god, who died and did not die, that son who was his own father by a virgin mother, a sacrifice of himself to Himself for sins that were not his. The continuity and timelessness of a personality is astonishing. We are, it seems, each one of us, the children of all historic mankind.

The Arunta, one of the Australian Bushmen tribes, have a provocative concept that they call "alchuringa time." Alchuringa time is the sacred heroic myth-time of the ancestors long long ago, when man and nature came to be what they are. It is "The Dreaming," now actually present in ritual; it was, and is, everywhen. Alchuringa time is the tribal eternity, as everlasting as tribal truth. It is found in dream, ritual, myth. The psychiatrist might term it the total impingement of past human lives on the life of an individual person. Alchuringa time is the past *now*, a formative still-creative phenomenon, made and making, the forgotten memory.

Alchuringa time is the timeless time of the unconscious mind. It is the childhood in us now, the immortal influence of dead others upon us. Alchuringa time is the group ethos of History; and, simultaneously, the alchuringa time of the individual is his character. In the reverberant nature of the social animal it is impossible to see where culture ends and character begins. For they are in origin the same: the formative influence of others upon us. Time is Koschei the Deathless "who made things as they are."

There is a neurological substrate to this psychic hardening of historic happenstance into emotional structure. Bok and Ariëns-Kappers have shown how in "stimulogenous fibrillation" the dendrites of a nerve cell actually grow along electrochemical vectors (like the hidden potential path of lightning) to become part of the permanent structure of the nerve cell — and then thereafter remain to govern all future experience of the network.[5]

The process goes even further. Categories imposed on stimuli from the infinitely varying outside world coalesce out of repetitive prejudged "likeness" of experiences, channeled through a merely finite number of brain cells. It is important to realize that "likeness" is a judgment; that is, a neural structure. For example, however varied these are objectively, all hexagonal crystals of frozen water-vapor are thenceforth "snowflake," and these categorical edicts become humanly immortal in a language, e.g., in the "starred form" of the Indo-European linguistic stock, thence to all its daughter languages for uncounted millennia. Thus "snowflake" snowballs from individual brain to the culture of a society, onward to human history at least as immortal as our genes. From stimulogenous fibrillation in a brain, to *Ursprache* and traditional culture, the word awesomely has become flesh.

Once grown, there seems to be no possible change in dendrites, for brain-cells are not replicable after an early age. The system is rigidly set in its ways. Only linguistic drift, functionally analogous to random mutation, may bring minute incremental change in meanings, but in either case, the causal chain remains unbroken. The human system is wasteful, as is all evolution, but change appears to lie only in individual metazoan death and arduous new social learning, in another new intricate and costly self-manufacturing computer. The only hope for change lies in the generation gap, in learning and genes alike. For in stimulogenous fibrillation, action becomes thing.

Anthropologists should see the relevance of neurological fact to all cultural history. There is cultural tyranny in all cognitive maps. One can not *think*, to the extent that all our thought is preprogrammed for us. Worse yet, the *first fall of the dice* pitilessly determines the rest of the game in all organic and hence cultural systems. Whatever occupies the psychic ground first becomes Culture, History. To change it then is no less difficult than to change a neurotic fixation. The scientist pioneers in the most modish thinking in the small area of his expertise, but only at the price of impiety to sacred culture; while he, in most other matters like the rest of us citizens, rests, comfortably or uncomfortably, in an old stone age of the mind whose momentum and inertia are incalculable. In the governance of human lives, there are not only neuroses and psychoses from individual childhoods but also group *archoses:* nonsense and misinformation so ancient and pervasive as to be seemingly inextricable from our thinking, a sacred ghost dance entrenched in the forgotten.

Notes

1. B. Bonnerjea, "Hunting Superstitions of the American Aborigines," *Internationales Archiv für Ethnographie,* (1934) 32(3 – 6):167 – 84; E. Lot-Falck, *Les rites de chasse chez les peuples sibériens* (Paris: Gallimard, 1953); M. G. Levin and L. P. Potapov, eds. *The Peoples of Siberia* (Chicago: University of Chicago Press, 1964), pp. 464, 649, 711, 757, 879; Caldua Chelius, "Knochen als Lebenskeime," Ph.D. dissertation, Hamburg University, 1962; and W. La Barre, *The Ghost Dance: Origins of Religion* (Garden City: Doubleday, 1970), pp. 167–69, 190n.14. So persistent is the concept of bone-regeneration that it is also applied to *plants.* "The ritual practice of leaving part of the [peyote] rootstalk in the ground to ensure new growth 'from Elder

Brother's [Deer's] bones' is common among Huichol peyote seekers." Peter Furst, *Hallucinogens and Culture* (San Francisco: Chandler and Sharp, 1976), p. 125. But of course the association of deer and hallucinogens — and of hallucinogens with the male principle—is itself of mesolithic antiquity. (The association of Elder Brother Deer specifically with peyote is Huichol.)

2. Ivar Paulson writes: "The animals themselves — as individual beings possessing power and souls and existing in their collective associations under the protection of the guardian spirit of the species—were probably among the oldest objects of the hunter's veneration; the game spirits and the game gods were perhaps the oldest divine spirits known to mankind... [for] the animal guardians are surely among the oldest theophanies in the religious life of mankind." Ivar Paulson, "The Animal Guardian: A Critical and Synthetic Review," *History of Religions*, (1964) 3:219. On the Master of Animals, see also W. La Barre, *Ghost Dance*, pp. 142 – 43, 153, 164, 190 – 91, nn10, 18 – 21.

3. "All known cultures derive eventually from a generalized Paleolithic culture." C. Kluckhohn, "Recurrent Themes in Myths and Mythmaking," in Alan Dundes, ed., *The Study of Folklore*, pp. 158 – 68 (Englewood Cliffs, N.J.: Prentice-Hall, 1965), p. 161; originally in *Daedalus*, (1959) 88:268–79. See also Kluckhohn's "Universal Categories in Culture," in A. L. Kroeber, ed., *Anthropology Today*, pp. 507 – 23 (Chicago: University of Chicago Press, 1953), p. 514; and André Varagnac, "L'archéocivilisation et le psychologie des peuples," *Revue de Psychologie des Peuples*, (1970) 25(1): 9 – 17.

This insight by cultural anthropologists is replicated by modern linguists. "[The method of lexicostatistics] served to convince Swadesh in later years not only of the community of origin of all languages but also of the existence of a common basic core in all human cultures that comes into being and perpetuates itself through human languages." Norman McQuown, in Swadesh Obituary, *American Anthropologist*, (1968) 70:756. Compare Sebeok: "The conclusions seem inescapable that the faculty of language—le langage — survived only once in the course of evolution, that its basic ground plan has remained both unaltered and peculiar to our species, and that the multiform language — les langues—concretely realized in human societies became differentiated from each other later on through the miscellaneous, more or less recognized, processes of historic linguistics... all known natural languages are relatively superficial variations on a single underlying theme." T. E. Sebeok, "Is a Comparative Semiotics Possible?" in Jean Pouillon and Pierre Maranda, eds., *Echanges et Communications: Málanges offerts à*

Claude Levi-Strauss, pp. 615 – 27, (2 vols.; [The Hague: Mouton, 1970], pp. 617 – 18).

4. The masculinizing effect of the *interstitial cells* of the testis — histologically distinct from the spermatogonia — was first demonstrated by P. Bouin and P. Ancel, "La glande interstituelle du testicule chez le cheval," *Archives zoologiques,* (1903) 3:391 ff, cited in Peter L. Williams and Roger Warwick, eds., *Gray's Anatomy,* 36th British ed. (Philadelphia: W. B. Saunders, 1980), p. 1415. No other function than the secretion of androgens can be attributed to Leydig's interstitial testicular cells, and no androgenous hormonal function to the spermatagonia.

5. S. T. Bok's "law of stimulogenous fibrillation," in C. U. Ariëns-Kappers, "On Structural Laws in the Nervous System," *Brain,* (1923) 44:132 – 33; Ariëns-Kappers' "law of neurobiotaxis," in "Further Contributions on Neurobiotaxis," *Journal of Comparative Neurology,* (1917) 27:266. A single human nerve cell may have up to 10,000 synapses, which trivializes anything a silicon chip can do.

CHAPTER I

From the Paleolithic
to the Protohistoric

The silent remains uncovered in archeological sites sometimes allow provocative inferences, but rarely any certainty. They are best presented in simple descriptions. One of the earliest and most tantalizing relevant sites is at Grosse Ofnet, Bavaria, a cave having an unbroken sequence from the lower Aurignacian (early Upper Old Stone Age) continuously through both Iron Ages into historic medieval times, such that there can be no question of serial position in time. Here, in the Azilian–Tardenoisean layer, were found two concentric circles, three feet apart, made up of six and twenty-seven human skulls respectively, with all the faces turned toward the west. Some of the skulls had upper vertebrae still attached, but with marks of forcible decapitation. The find was not a simple burial of the dead (for only the thirty-three skulls were present) but rather a ritual sacrifice, having a seemingly intentional reference to the direction of the setting sun. In 1937 another such nest was found in the Höhlenstein cave near Württemberg, both male and female skulls showing fractures as from a heavy blow, and marks of decapitation on the cervical vertebrae. Breuil and Lantier found the skull cult throughout the entire Upper Paleolithic; Glory and Robert a culte des crânes humains in prehistoric epochs; and Wernert compared paleolithic with contemporary headhunting among primitive tribes, as also did Pinza.[1]

More than simple head-burial is evidenced in numerous other sites. Blanc[2] concluded that the mutilation of the base of the skull in the Monte Circeo, Ehringsdorf, and Steinheim skulls indicated the practice of eating human brains by early and late Neanderthals for about 250,000 years. Blanc also pointed out that body-cannibalism was well known in the Mousterian period; Krapina would be the classic European site. Bourgounioux,[3] with the concurrence of Carl Sauer, suggested that Neanderthal headhunting was for this cannibal purpose. As to the range of such brain-eating, it is highly suggestive that over forty specimens of Neanderthaloid "Peking Man" at Choukoutien were represented by skulls and skull fragments but by very few limb bones—a proportion which Blanc believes points strongly to headhunting also in ancient China.[4] Blanc connects burials of skulls in Upper Paleolithic and Mesolithic sites in Europe (Arcy-sur-Curé and Placard, as well as Ofnet) with pictorial evidence of ritual slaughter from engravings in the Upper Paleolithic cave of Addauro (Palermo).[5] The Ertebølle people, from indications at Dyrholmen (East Jutland), after scalping a decapitated human head, seem also to have eaten the brains.[6]

Headhunting for the purpose of eating the brain survived in late European prehistory into the Bronze Age, as shown in the "Bell Beaker" skull from Wansleben, Saxony, the base of which Gerhardt proved had been intentionally mutilated; a similar one is known from the immediately following "Frühahnjetitser" culture in Saxony.[7] Headhunting survived in Britain into protohistoric times (Catuvellauni in Hertfordshire, and among other tribes elsewhere in Britain), and in France Celtic Iron Age headhunting lasted into historic times.[8] A pre – Iron Age cult of the skull has actually survived in fragments among the Slavs until the second decade of the present century.[9]

What might we conservatively conclude concerning these Old Stone Age practices? That there was a very ancient belief in human life-power apparently resident especially in the skull, to be obtained by eating the brains of other men. Sergio Sergi carefully studied the

Monte Circeo I skull of a Neanderthal, which had a deliberate breaking away of the bone at the base of the skull around the foramen magnum; Vallois saw similarity with practices in recent African tribes; and Blanc adduced a skull from the d'Entrecasteaux Islands of Melanesia with mutilation almost identical with that of the Monte Circeo skull. From his exhaustive study of the Ehringsdorf skull, Weidenreich concluded that the individual was killed by a stone weapon striking the frontal region and that the absence of a cranial base indicated that the skull was then intentionally opened to extract the brain.[10] Berckhemer confirmed the conclusions of Sergi and Weidenreich through his work on the Steinheim skull, discovered in 1932.[11] Von Koenigswald pointed out the similarity of mutilation in the eleven skulls that he and Ter Haar discovered in 1931 at Ngandong to those made on skulls by recent Borneo headhunters in the same region; indeed, the arrangement of the Ngandong skulls was like that of the late-Paleolithic skulls at Ofnet.[12]

The Celts provide the first massive evidence of headhunting in Europe, which dates from the late prehistoric to the pre-Roman protohistoric period. The Celtic-speaking peoples once ranged in a broad east-west band from Galatia in Phrygia (Asia Minor) over northern Italy and central Europe into Gaul. Ross writes of "the universal Celtic cult of the head":[13] "The theme of the head... goes right through Celtic religious tradition and is found, not only as a separate cult, but bound up with all other cults. The horned god likewise appears in association with the cult of the warrior gods and the theme of the head.[14] Ross cites Ofnet as a Mesolithic forerunner of the developed head cult in the same area.[15] The Celts were an "Urn Field" people and were related to both the La Tène and Hallstadt Iron Ages, their widespread symbol being the ram-headed snake of their god of war.[16]

The human head is given first place as being the most typical Celtic religious symbol. The human head was regarded by the Celts as being symbolic of divinity and otherworld powers. The motif of the sacred head figures

throughout the entire field of Celtic cult practice, temporally and geograph-
ically, and it can be traced in both representational and literary contexts
from the very beginning to the latter part of the tradition. [17]

Ross believes "the evidence strongly suggests that the Celtic cult of
the head stems direct from Urnfield and earlier Bronze Age Europe
where the head was clearly used in certain instances as a solar
symbol" [18] — a circumstance which perhaps illuminates the orien-
tation to the west of the Ofnet and other skull circles. [19] Certainly the
head cult was well entrenched. Cunliffe writes that "The Celtic head
cult probably has very ancient origins. The early prehistoric inhabitants of eastern France, in sites such as [the] cave in the 'Dame
Jouanne' hills (Seine-et-Loire), practiced a severed-head cult long
before the Celts." [20]

We know that the proto-historic Celts were quite specifically *head
hunters* in their wars, for their cult of the head is well-documented
in classic sources. Diodorus Siculus wrote that

they cut off the heads of enemies slain in battle and attach them to the necks
of their horses. The blood-stained spoils they hand over to their attendants
and carry off as a booty while striking up a paean and singing a song of
victory; and they nail up these first fruits upon their houses. . . . They embalm
in cedar oil the heads of the most distinguished enemies, and preserve them
carefully in a chest and display them with pride to strangers, saying that for
this head one of their ancestors, or his father, or the man himself refused the
offer of a large sum of money. They say that some of them boast that they
refused the weight of the head in gold. [21]

Powell warns that "It would be hazardous to dismiss this custom
amongst the Celts as being merely a desire to collect trophies for the
accumulation of martial prestige," and he considers the cult related
to human fertility and to power and ownership of the enemy spirit. [22]
Celts valued the head extremely because the head enclosed the life-
stuff. As Cunliffe writes, "The head symbolized the very essence of
being, and consequently could exist in its own right. By possessing
someone's head, one controlled that person and his spirit. These

beliefs are manifest in the archeological evidence, the classical tradition, and the Irish and Welsh literature."[23]

The Latin historian Livy wrote of events in the third century B.C. concerning a catastrophic Roman defeat by the Celts: "The Consuls got no report of the disaster until some Gallic horsemen came in sight, with heads hanging at their horses' breasts, or fixed on their lances, and singing their customary songs of triumph."[24] The account refers to the aftermath of an ambush by the Boii, a Celtic tribe then occupying part of the Po valley in northern Italy, where the Roman consul-elect Lucius Postumius was killed. The Boii "stripped his body, cut off his head, and carried their spoils in triumph to the most hallowed of their temples. There they cleaned out the head, as is their custom, and gilded the skull, which thereafter served them as a holy vessel to pour libations from and as a drinking cup for their priests and temple attendants."[25] The heads of lesser figures were placed on stakes, that their power might protect a fortress.

On Trajan's Column in Rome is carved just such a Celtic fort, the heads on stakes here being those of Roman soldiers captured by the Dacians in Transylvania.[26] A triumphal arch at Orange in the Vaucluse, dating from the second half of the first century B.C. also shows decapitated heads, and on some of the trophy shields there are Celtic proper names.[27] The general inspiration is the trophy friezes at Pergamon, such influences coming through an ancient colony of Magna Graecia at nearby Marsala (Marseille); but the Orange sculpture is not a copy of the Greek, since Roman and Gallic weapons of the appropriate period can be identified.

The most striking archeological evidence of the Celtic cult of severed heads is found in two pre-Roman temples in southern France, Entremont and Roqueperteuse. Entremont, at Aix-en-Provence near the mouth of the Rhône, dates from the Celtic Iron Age of the third and second centuries B.C. Strabo ranked this capital of the Celtic Saluvii tribe as a *polis;* it was destroyed in 123 – 124 B.C. The hill-fortress *(oppidum),* covering some nine acres, had streets of single-room houses within a bastioned stone wall; a sanctuary of the severed-head cult was found at the highest point of the hill. Within the shrine was a tall pillar with twelve simplified human heads; Piggott shows photographs of the stone pillar, reused as a threshold, dating from the La Tène period at the middle of the second century B.C.[28] Entremont provides many examples of "têtes coupées" sculptured in blocks of stone.[29] Although some show evidence of Greek influence from Massilia (Marseille), the hair of both sexes is dressed in Celtic style; there are individual carvings of men, women, and children, as well as groups of heads.

In the portico of the celebrated temple of Roqueperteuse, niches were carved to hold human heads — several of which are still held in place as skulls by the masonry, though Roman colonists destroyed the sanctuary itself in the late second century A.D. An actual human skull peers from a niche of a stone pillar of the sanctuary from Roqueperteuse, now in the Musée Borély, Marseille.[30] The Roqueperteuse skulls are all of males under forty and were dedicated to the Gallic war-god Taranis. A third evidence of the head cult is the famed *Tarasque* at Noves in southern France, a fearsome scaly monster devouring a corpse and holding two severed human heads, one in each forepaw (third to second century B.C.)[31] Together, Entremont, Roqueperteuse, and the Noves monster indicate remarkable strength of the Celtic head cult in the hinterland of Marseille.

Although Celts, driven out of Gaul by Caesar's legions, appear in some places to have brought the cult of severed heads with them, Ross plausibly considers headhunting to be pre-Celtic in the British Isles.[32] On the one hand (arguing for importation): Cunobelinus, about A.D. 10, founded in Hertfordshire his capital Camulodunum, "fortress of Camulos," named for a war god brought with the Celts from northeastern France; and his Catuvellauni raided neighboring kingdoms in Britain for both slaves and human heads, "accepted respectively as the profit and proof of martial prowess."[33] On the other hand (arguing for indigenous occurrence): similarly to the

Impernal *oppidum* of the Cadurci near Cahors in the Rhône valley, where skulls were nailed into position, at the Bredon (Gloucestershire) Iron Age fort, skulls decorated the lintel of the gateway, to be brought crashing down when the defenses were raided and burned in the early first century A.D.[34] At Stanwick, in Yorkshire, a skull had been nailed over a gate. At Danebury, in northern Britain, skulls have been found on the bottom of food storage pits. Because of the deep-seated Celtic belief in the head as the literal seat of fertility, Cunliffe considers these to be connected with a successful harvest.[35] In addition, "Fragments of skulls have been found amid the domestic remains of a number of settlements, often worn smooth by handling and occasionally perforated so that they could be worn as amulets."[36] The use of heads as protective apotropaic gargoyles to ward off noxious spirits is well established. On a horned head from Lanchester, County Durham, Ross remarks that "the treatment of the mouth with its slightly protruding tongue is reminiscent of certain of the Irish monuments."[37] (Interestingly, on a Roman fort in Hungary, there is a stone head with a thrust-out tongue, although here a derisive defiance may be added to the ancient apotropaic gesture.)[38]

In a Celtic context a horned human head would appear remarkably redundant, since for Celts both head and horn symbolize fertility directly. The principal "horned god" of the Celts is Cernunnus, antlered lord of animal fertility and master of animals, and (like Roman Pluto) an underground god of spirits and wealth. The antler-crowned shaman is of Old Stone Age antiquity in France (e.g., the Dancing Sorcerer of Trois Frères); a Cernunnus is shown on the Celtic Gundestrup Cauldron. Cernunnus appears in the central stronghold of Celtic culture, that of the Parisii in the Ile de la Cité, under the cathedral of Notre Dame, and in that of Reims; there is even a statue of Cernunnus from Roqueperteuse.[39] But the springing of male antlers directly from brain-*muelos* is quite to be expected, given the ancient placing of the life-stuff itself in the head. "The yearly growth of stag antlers and the obvious connection with the sexual cycle suggest fertility and reproductive potency; the autumnal shedding and spring regrowth further imply seasonal rebirth and immortality in nature. That horns symbolize life force is unmistakable from the heaps of red deer antlers piled on Tardenoisean graves on the islands of Hoëdic and Téviec near Quiberan (Morbihan)."[40] These finds are of the Mesolithic period, but are not to be confused with the Maglemosian of Star Carr hunters in use or meaning.

Some of the dead in the Téviec rockbuilt tombs wore antler headdresses, and the custom of piling antlers on tombs persisted into the Bronze Age in Britain, e.g., at Three Hills, Mildenhall (Suffolk), where eighteen fine red deer antlers were heaped over a primary burial. That the Three Hills burial was of a woman and burial D at Téviec of a woman and child both strongly suggest the motifs of life force, rebirth and immortality, since women and children are not deer hunters — an interpretation moreover consistent with the widespread use of red ochre in graves and in several cave grottoes. In fact, the fertility motif is still found in the yearly Horn Dance of country folk at Abbots Bromley in Staffordshire, when staghorns are ritually carried in a seasonal ceremony.[41]

Antlers and horns growing directly from the *muelos*-containing head are to be taken literally as fertility symbols, though the country folk of Abbots Bromley were only dimly aware of the symbolic significance of their ritual.

The head as repository of the *muelos* – semen is strikingly illustrated by a figurine from Tongres:

In 1942 Lambrechts published an important bronze statuette from Tongres. The figure is seated and holds a purse in the right hand [in both of these features like the typical Cernunnus] and a bird in the left hand [a common familiar or messenger of a god or shaman]. The figure was originally *triphallic*. The penis has disappeared but a phallus is placed on the top of the head and the nose is likewise replaced by a phallus. The phallus on the head has a small trough for suspension. Lambrechts lists other figures having phalloi coming from their heads.... The association of the phallus with the head is important here.[42]

Ross mentions "the traditional Celtic association between the head and the phallus" and, again, "the funerary association of the head and the phallus." Esperandieu also shows a figure (no. 2132) carrying two phalli, and Ross believes that this "Celtic Mercury clearly averted evil spirits" and assimilates it to a male figure in the Camelon Collection in the National Museum of Scotland.[43] (The head as glans of the body-as-phallus is also a very old visual trope in Indo-European iconography: compare European examples of great age with the traditional Indic Shiva producing the river Ganges from the top of his head.)[44] It would be difficult to be more explicit. Only willful denial could ignore the multiply insistent symbolism.

As Cunliffe observes, "The head remained a powerful motif throughout the Christian period in Ireland and indeed in the rest of Europe. The gargoyles, corbels, and other decorative heads which decorate many churches, particularly of the eleventh to twelfth centuries A.D., owe much to the Celtic interpretation of the head. Often it is impossible to distinguish Celtic from Christian carvings."[45] For example, at Dysert O'Dea in Ireland, carved in a stone arch over a doorway, are eleven severed heads; in the tympanum over the arched church doorway at Clonfert are ten heads in triangular niches; and below this are five more heads in arcade. Both are of Romanesque date and style.

The same syncretism of Celtic and Christian symbolism appears at the diagonally opposite end of Europe in northern Italy. The Celts of Lake Como, probably akin to the headhunting Boii of the adjacent Po valley, left many archeological remains, especially plentiful on the anciently fortified promontory of Bellagio.[46] At Gravedona, northward a few miles on the western shore of the lake, and opposite an early Formative Romanesque Lombard church, there is a curious war memorial, the lavish decoration of which with skulls and crossbones forcibly recalls the transalpine sanctuaries of Entremont and Roqueperteuse in southern France (Gravedona being about midway between the Po and the Rhône). The context of the memorial suggests that the traditional Christian motif of skull and crossbones is here not so much a lugubrious *memento mori* as it is an assertion of the magical immortality of heroes in war. If so, this is consistent with a Celtic symbolism that is millennia old.

The evidence is not solely archeological. "The cult of the severed head is a concurrent theme in the Irish literature. The hero Cu Chulainn, by the end of his exploits, had an enormous collection to his credit."[47] Not only is the head the reservoir of the life-stuff but, like the head of the shaman – bard Orpheus cast up on the island of Lesbos, the head had a continuing life of its own, and whoever possessed it possessed its power. The legend of the speaking head is widespread. In a Norse legend, Odin took the head of the decapitated Mimir and treated it with oil and herbs, so that it became capable of speech and told many secret matters to the god and would prophesy.[48] In an early Irish story, *Cath Almaine*, "The head of Fergus Mac Máile Dúin is washed, braided and combed, and a silken cloth is put upon it. Offerings are then made to it, upon which it speaks."[49] There is a tale of the decapitated head of St. Melos speaking.[50] "The cult of the severed head is also reflected in the Welsh literature. In the *Mabinogion* the severed head of the god Bran goes on actively directing events long after it has been removed from its wounded body."[51] (The motif of the speaking head is also African, Asiatic, and American Indian.)

The head having contained the life essence, the skull cap was also appropriate for drinking from. The practice is evidently ancient. In the Solutrean and Magdalenian (Upper Paleolithic) levels in the Grotte du Placard, skull tops were found which Breuil and Obermaier thought were used for drinking; one of the best of the Placard cups shows traces of red ochre, a well-known Paleolithic symbol for blood – fire – life.[52] Such skull cups have also been found from Upper Paleolithic Castilla (northern Spain) all the way to Unter-Winternitz (Moravia). Maringer notes human skulls converted into drinking cups found in Swiss Lake Dwelling sites and in French burial places of the Neolithic period.[53]

Imbibing from skull cups is also established ethnographically and historically.

Herodotus wrote that the "Issedones" (?Tibetans) drank from the gold-mounted skulls of their ancestors, and the thirteenth-century missionary William of Ruysbrook wrote the same of Tibetans; James Rennel saw finely lacquered human skull cups in Bengal. Plutarch wrote that ancient Teutons drank from the skulls of their bravest enemies to imbibe their courage; so too did the Scythians. Even medieval Christians made cups of skulls of slain foes; for example, in 880 A.D. the Bulgarian prince Krum had a cup made of the skull of the Byzantine Emperor Nicephorus II. [54]

The motive was not degradation of the enemy or revenge upon him, but serious magic for the benefit of the drinker. "In 1875, a skull was found at Pompeii, mounted in precious metals and with the inscription in Greek, "Drink and you shall live for many years" — as if longevity could be increased by imbibing life-stuff. In fact, there is much evidence that the *contents* of the 'cup,' the brain *muellos* or skull 'marrow' was the life source and seed itself." [55] Here, to drink life (eau de vie, whiskey—both, literally, "water of life") is to prolong it; hence the familiar toasts "to your health" or "salud" and the like —although purists consider that only the hostess who offers it should propose "skoal" (skull).

Indeed, the equation of "cup" and "skull" is so universal in the daughter languages that this metaphor must go back to the original undivided Indo-European stock, which would give us a date ranging from the Chalcolithic to the early Bronze Age.

Italian *coppa* is also "cup," but the cognate Provençal *cobs* is "skull." It might also be pointed out that Greek κεφαλή and Anglo-Saxon *hafala* agree with the Sanskrit *kapāla,* which means both cup and skull; that in the Germanic languages *Kopf* and cup are cognates; that the Scandinavian *skoal* means drinking bowl, like the Scottish *skull,* a bowl or goblet for liquor; and that even the French *tête* from late Latin slang means a pottery bowl. Such consistency in Indoeuropean languages suggests more than mere poetic metaphor. Apparently the "genius" of a man could be obtained by eating or drinking it. [56]

Indeed, the philologist Onians gives many examples of the overlap or the identity of *genius* and *genital* words in the Indo-European languages and explains why the seed of grain is in its "head," why from Plautus onward the source of a stream is its "head," and why the generative force and genius alike are thought to be in the head.[57] The term *cerebrum* comes from the old verb *cereo (creo),* "I beget, create" (compare Ceres, "head," goddess of grain, and *cerus,* "engenderer"); *sapere* "to know" means to hold native juice. The thighbone, *femur,* is the "marrow bone" par excellence, from the root *fe-,* whence *fetus, fecundus, femina.* A man's *genius* (feminine *juno*) is his personality and capacity for pleasure, but originally meant the generative potency resident in his head (and, for peculiar reasons, in his *genus,* "jaw," and *genu,* "knee").[58] Professor Rose writes that

the *genius* is the life, or reproductive power, almost the luck, of the family, appearing as is usual with the Roman manifestations of *mana* in a masculine and a feminine form, naturally appropriated to the male and female heads of the house. . . . The *genius* then is .one, and one only, for each family, and probably originally only one for each *gens.* . . . [The *genius* and *iuno*] were spirits belonging to no individual alive or dead but to the clan.[59]

But here we have come back again to the Old Stone Age conception of a "master of animals." The *genius* is none other than he.

Notes

1. H. Breuil and R. Lantier, *Les hommes de la pierre ancienne* (Paris: Payot, 1951), pp. 289ff. A. Glory and R. Robert, "Le culte des crânes humains aux époques préhistoriques," *Bulletin de la Société d'Anthropologie de Paris* (1948), 53:114 – 33. P. Wernert, "L'anthropophagie rituelle de la chasse aux têtes aux époques actuelles et Paléolithique," *L'Anthropologie* (1936) 33 – 43, and "Culte des crânes: Représentation des esprits des défunts et des ancêtres," pp. 50 – 102 in M. Gorce and R. Mortier, eds., *L'histoire générale des religions* (Paris: Quillet, 1948); G. Pinza, "La conservazione delle teste e i costumi con i quali si connette," *Memorie della Società geografica italiana,* vol. 7, no. 2. See also Teuku Jacob, "The Problem of Head-Hunting and Brain-Eating Among Pleistocene Men in Indonesia," *Archaeology and Physical Anthropology in Oceania,* (1972), 7(2):81 – 91.

2. A. C. Blanc, "Some Evidences for the Ideologies of Early Man," in S. L. Washburn, ed., *Social Life of Early Man,* pp. 123 – 32. Viking Fund Publications in Anthropology no. 31 (New York, 1961).

3. F. M. Bourgounioux, "'Spiritualité' de l'Homme Neanderthal," in G. H. R. von Koenigswald, ed., *Hundert Jahre Neanderthaler*, pp. 151 – 66 (Utrecht: Kemink en Zoon, 1958).

4. André Senet, *Man in Search of his Ancestors* (New York: McGraw-Hill, 1956), pp. 113 – 14. Bed II *Homo erectus* at Olduvai already has this artificially enlarged foramen magnum! — which Philip Tobias associates with Blanc's evidence for brain-eating. Personal communication, April 8, 1968.

5. See W. La Barre, *The Ghost Dance: Origins of Religion* (New York: Doubleday, 1970), p. 428 n. 48, for prehistoric human sacrifice.

6. Blanc, "Some Evidences," p. 123; O. Klindt-Jensen, *Denmark Before the Vikings* (London: Thames and Hudson, 1957), pp. 36 – 37.

7. K. Gerhardt, "Künstliche Veränderungen am Hinterhauptloch vorgeschichtlicher Schädel," *Germania* (1951), 29:3 – 4.

8. I. A. Richmond, *Roman Britain* (Baltimore: Penguin Books, 1960), pp. 11 – 13; in Gaul, cf. pp. 192 – 93; T. G. E. Powell, *The Celts* (New York: Praeger, 1958), pp. 108, 110, plates 50 – 51; Stuart Piggott, *Ancient Europe, from the Beginnings of Agriculture to Classical Antiquity* (Chicago: Aldine, 1965), plate 38; also pp. 223, 230, 259. For the Gundestrup Cauldron, probably Celtic, see Ole Klindt-Jensen, *Gundestrupkedelen* (Copenhagen: Nationalmuseet, 1961), figs. 4 – 5; G. G. MacCurdy, *Human Origins*, 2 vols. (New York: Johnson Reprint Corporation, 1965), figs. 384, 385.

9. Evel Gasparini, "Studies in Old Slavic Religion: *Ubrus*," *History of Religions* (1962), 2:112 – 39.

10. F. Wiegers, F. Weidenreich, and E. Schuster, *Der Schädelfund von Weimar-Ehringsdorf* (Jena: Fischer, 1928).

11. F. Berckhemer, "Der Steinheimer Urmensch und die Tierwelt seines Lebensgebietes," *Naturwissenschaftliche Monatschrift der Deutschen Naturkundverein* (Stuttgart), (1934), 47:4.

12. La Barre, *Ghost Dance*, pp. 404 – 5; Max Ebert, *Reallexikon der Vorgeschichte* (Berlin: Gruyter, 1927), 9:162; Anne Ross, *Pagan Celtic Britain* (London: Kegan Paul, 1967), p. 62.

13. Ross, *Pagan Celtic Britain*, p. 6.

14. Ross, *Pagan Celtic Britain*, p. 61; Ross, "The Human Head in Insular Celtic Religion," *Proceedings of the Society of Antiquarians of Scotland* (1957 – 1958), 91:10 – 43; Ross, "Severed Heads in Wells: An Aspect of the Head Cult," *Scottish Studies* (1962), 6:31 – 48. See also P. Lambrechts, *L'exaltation de la tête dans la pensée et dans l'art des Celtes* (Bruges, Belgium: De Tempel, 1954); Lambrechts, *Contribution à l'étude des divinités celtiques*, (Bruges: De Tempel, 1942).

15. Ross, *Pagan Celtic Britain*, p. 62.
16. Ross, *Pagan Celtic Britain*, p. 9.
17. Ross, *Pagan Celtic Britain*, p. 61.
18. Ross, *Pagan Celtic Britain*, pp. 9, 62.
19. Ross, *Pagan Celtic Britain*, p. 62. See also Kathleen Kenyon, *Archaeology in the Holy Land* (New York: Praeger, 1960), plate 13, p. 76.
20. B. Cunliffe, *The Celtic World* (New York: McGraw-Hill, 1979), p. 84; see also J. A. MacCulloch, *The Religion of the Ancient Celts* (Edinburgh: Clark, 1911), p. 34; cf. pp. 240ff, 337; and R. B. Onians, *The Origins of European Thought* (New York: Arno Press, 1973), pp. 100–1, 156, 236.
21. Diodorus Siculus, xiv, 115; Strabo, iv, 11.4; Livy, x, 26, in Cunliffe, *The Celtic World*, p. 83. Herodotus writes that the Scythian Tauri impaled the heads of all those shipwrecked on their Black Sea shores. "As for the enemies they overcome, each man cuts off his enemy's head and carries it away to his house where he impales it on a tall pole and sets it standing high above the dwelling, above the smoke-vent for the most part. These heads, they say, are set aloft to guard the whole house." Herodotus, iv, 103, A. D. Godley, trans., 4 vols. (New York: Putnam, 1928), 2:305, 307. Aeneas fought Rutulians in Latium who impaled enemy heads on spears (*Aeneid* 9:465 – 67, 471 – 72).
22. Powell, *The Celts*, p. 108.
23. Cunliffe, *The Celtic World*, p. 83.
24. Livy, x, 26.
25. Livy, in Cunliffe, *The Celtic World*, p. 83.
26. Cunliffe, *The Celtic World*, p. 83; Ross, *Pagan Celtic Britain*, p. 66.
27. Powell, *The Celts*, plates 50, 51, pp. 266–67.
28. Piggott, *Ancient Europe*, plate 38, p. 219; F. Benoit, *L'art primitif Méditerranéen de la Valée du Rhône* (Paris: Ophrys, 1955).
29. Ross, *Pagan Celtic Britain*, figs. 25–28, pp. 65–66; F. Benoit, *Entremont: Capitale Celto-ligure des Salyens de Provence* (1957).
30. Roqueperteuse skull, Musée Borély, Marseilles; photograph in Geoffrey Bibby, "The Mysterious Celts," in J. J. Thorndike, Jr., ed., *Discovery of Lost Worlds*, pp. 174–83 (New York: American Heritage, 1979), p. 184; Piggott, *Ancient Europe*, p. 230.
31. Cunliffe, *The Celtic World*, p. 84.
32. Ross, *Pagan Celtic Britain*, p. 65. Cf. Piggot, *Ancient Europe*, p. 259.
33. Richmond, *Roman Britain*, pp. 11–13.
34. Impernal: Benoit, *Entremont*, pp. 22–23; M. A. Cotton, "British Camps with Timber-laced Ramparts," *Archaeological Journal*, (1955),

111:26–105. Bredon: T. C. Hencken, "The Excavations of the Iron Age Camp on Bredon Hill," *Archaeological Journal* (1938), 95:1 – 111.

35. Cunliffe, *The Celtic World*, p. 83.

36. Cunliffe, *The Celtic World*, p. 83.

37. Ross, *Pagan Celtic Britain*, p. 82.

38. W. La Barre, *Culture in Context: Selected Papers* (Durham, N.C.: Duke University Press, 1980), pp. 298 – 99.

39. La Barre, *Ghost Dance*, pp. 416, 430.

40. La Barre, *Ghost Dance*, pp. 414, 429 – 30.

41. La Barre, *Ghost Dance*, p. 414; M. and S. – J. Péquart, M. Boule, and H. V. Valois, *Téviec, station nécropole mésolithique du Morbihan* (Paris: Masson, 1937); M. Péquart and S. – J. Péquart, "Le nécropole mésolithique de Téviec," *L'Anthropologie* (1929) 39: 373 – 400; Péquart and Péquart, *Hoëdic, deuxième station-nécropole du mésolithique côtier Armorican* (Anvers: De Sikkel, 1954).

42. Ross, *Pagan Celtic Britain*, p. 93 n. 3.

43. Ross, *Pagan Celtic Britain*, pp. 93, 103; Ross, "The Human Head in Pagan Celtic Religion," *Proceedings of the Society of Antiquaries of Scotland* (1959), 92:28.

44. Ross, *Pagan Celtic Britain*, p. 93. Cf. "In phantasies and in numerous symptoms the head too appears as a symbol of the male genitals, or, if one prefers to put it so, as something standing for them" (S. Freud, *Standard Edition* [1959], 14:339).

45. Cunliffe, *The Celtic World*, p. 86.

46. John Marshall, *The Castle's Keep: The Villa Serbelloni in History* (ms., 2 vols., 1970, Library, Rockefeller Foundation Villa Serbelloni, Bellagio, Lake Como, Italy). See also B. Olson, *The Point that Divides the Wind* (Menaggio: privately printed, n.d.); Carlos Ferrario, *Lake of Como Villas and Gardens* (Como: Brunner, 1980).

47. Cunliffe, *The Celtic World*, p. 84.

48. *Ynglinga Saga*, ch. 4; *Heimskringla* (1941), 1:12 – 13, 18; *Edda Snorra* (Sturlusunar, 1931); *Völuspa*, stanzas 28 and 46; Sigrdrifumal 13, in Ross, *Pagan Celtic Britain*, p. 109.

49. Ross, *Pagan Celtic Britain*, p. 111.

50. Ross, *Pagan Celtic Britain*, p. 109.

51. Cunliffe, *The Celtic World*, p. 86.

52. J. Maringer, *The Gods of Prehistoric Man* (London: Weiderfeld & Nicolson, 1960), p. 54; Ross, *Pagan Celtic Britain*, p. 62, La Barre, *Ghost Dance*, p. 407.

53. Maringer, *The Gods of Prehistoric Man*, p. 178.

54. La Barre, *Ghost Dance*, p. 406.

55. Maringer, *The Gods of Prehistoric Man*, pp. 55–56, in La Barre, *Ghost Dance*, pp. 406, 428.

56. La Barre, *Ghost Dance*, pp. 406, 428 n. 57.

57. Onians, *Origins*, pp. 93–167.

58. For the etymologies of these words, see Onians, *Origins*: cerebrum-cereo-cerus, pp. 125 and n 8, 148, 150, 238, 240, n 7, 244; sapere, pp. 61–63, 65; femur-fetus-fecundus-femina, p. 182; genius, p. 127, citing Birt (see also Onians' General Index s.v.); genus-genu, pp. 175–76, 180–81, 233.

59. H. J. Rose, "On the Original Significance of the *Genius*," *Classical Quarterly*, (1923), 17:59ff; Rose, "Ancient Italian Beliefs Concerning the Soul," *Classical Quarterly* (1930), 24:135, in Onians, *Origins*, p. 128.

CHAPTER II

Ethnographic: Old World

Headhunting for brain-eating purposes is not only known among Neanderthaloids of the Old Stone Age from Bavaria to China (and in Pleistocene Indonesia); and enemy head-collecting not only persisted in central and western Europe among Iron Age Celts (and perhaps Bronze Age Indo-Europeans at large); but indications of the ancient *muelos* superstition — the head as site of fertility — is well known also from the ethnographic present. I do not intend to present here a comprehensive survey of worldwide headhunting, but to sample instances to show the remarkable similarity of meaning, whether in southeastern Asia, Indonesia, and Melanesia or in the Americas. Recent twentieth-century fieldwork tends to give the fullest accounts, although excellent reports are available from the last century for both the Old and New Worlds.

The human head, especially that of high-ranking persons, has a special place in Polynesia. The head of a man in a long series of first-born lineages is peculiarly sacred, for in the head of this living god is embodied the fertility of all the noble ancestors. An elaborately tatooed head is especially valued among the Maori of New Zealand, not solely for esthetic reasons but because only the high-ranking can afford the repeated and expensive process of tattooing, which thus constitutes a visible billboard of social prestige. For the same reason of rank, commoners crouch or sit down in the presence of the highborn. No man dares stand higher than the head of the high chief, since within it lies his formidable *mana* and powerful taboo-placing potency. A related notion is that the magician – craftsman (*tuhuna*) with his sacred knowledge engenders and creatively builds some-thing new into the structure of the universe with his chants when making, say, a new war-canoe.

Competitive headhunting to collect soul-stuff thought to be in the head is widespread in mainland southeastern Asia (notably in Assam and in the Wa States of Burma) and in Indonesia — from the Batak of Sumatra and Dyak of Borneo to the aboriginals of Taiwan and the Philippines — as well as in Melanesia and New Guinea.[1] Among the peoples of northern Assam, Gerald Berreman emphasizes the great importance of raiding and defense among villages and the impor-tance of "soul matter" "obtained from human victims through head-hunting or allied practices to assure the vitality and fertility of village members."[2] Earlier, however, a more generalized concern for fertility is evident in the Naga hills, according to J. H. Hutton: "The under-lying purpose" in head-hunting is to secure the "fertilizing soul-matter" which resides in the human head and is able to fructify crops."[3] Onians, citing St. John, writes that "the Dyak…hunted heads in the belief that they were supremely sources of fertility."[4] Among the Land Dyaks of Borneo, a newly taken head is thought. "to make their rice grow well, to cause the forest to abound with wild animals, to make their dogs and snares to be successful in securing game, to have the streams swarm with fish, to give health and activity to the people themselves, and to ensure the fertility of the women."[5] In fact, in his important paper on "Severed Heads that Germinate," Freeman noted that among the Rungus Dusun of North Borneo, an infertile woman is treated by having a trophy head placed between her thighs.

Berreman writes that in Assam "these practices have been aban-doned by most groups," nevertheless, during the Second World War, allied agents gave bounties on Japanese heads but not on those of American airmen downed in the India-China Hump region. In the 1940s, toward the end of the war in the Pacific (when many heads were taken by the Iban of Sarawak), the Australian anthropologist

Freeman witnessed several of the spectacular *gawai* ceremonies, "the central rite of which symbolizes the splitting of the head by Lang Singalang Burang, Iban god of war, and the release of 'seed.'[6] Indeed, when the British abolished headhunting, the Eddystone Islanders responded with despair. As Rivers wrote, "By stopping the practice of head-hunting the new (i.e., British) rulers were abolishing an institution which had its roots in the religious life of the people. The natives have responded to that by becoming apathetic. They have ceased to increase sufficiently to prevent the diminution of the island's population."[7] Among the Angami Naga, "the younger men complain bitterly that the British, by stopping their raids and so preventing them from getting marks of distinction, have made it impossible for them to get wives."[8]

The default, however, is not simply a deprivation of opportunities for displaying prowess but a far more fundamental matter. Maleness is thought to be a fixed *quantity* of substance, not a quality, and headhunting is imperative because of a "zero sum" ideology. Sexuality depletes total tribal vitality, and therefore young men must collect enemy heads to replenish the sum. A man must therefore take an enemy head before he may marry. In his *History of Human Marriage*, Westermarck writes that "of the Atagals of Formosa, the Gadanes of Luzon, the Alfoors of Ceram, the Dyaks of Borneo, and the Nagas of Upper Assam, it is reported that no man can marry without having first procured at least one human head.[9]

This was not a mere token of valor, as with a Sea Dyak chief, but connected with physical adolescence itself. "As to the hill tribes of Assam, Mr. Hodson is inclined to believe that success in headhunting was at one time, if not essential to marriage, regarded at least as a token of having passed from adolescence to maturity."[10] The concept of generic *fertility* contained in heads would suggest that we take the Naga literally: for them *heads contain seed*.

On the matter of trophies, it is difficult to be more specific than the Galla: "The desire of a Galla warrior is to deprive the enemy of his genitals, the possession of such a trophy being said to be a necessary preliminary to marriage."[11] According to Waitz, the Abyssinians and all the neighboring Hamitic peoples cut off the genitals of slain enemies.[12] The same usage obtained among all the Kaffir tribes.[13] It occurred also in Polynesia, the Solomon Islands of Melanesia, and in Papua.[14] The ancient Egyptians collected male genitals in their battles, and something like this is recorded of biblical Hebrews.[15] The practice was even sporadic in Europe. After the famous "vespers," the Sicilians "cut off the private parts of the hated strangers, and sent a whole shipload of these tokens to France."[16] The custom was early Welsh also.[17] Revenge, humiliation of the enemy, and other mixed motives are doubtless present in many of these practices, though such trophies are commonly proofs of manly prowess in warfare and not everywhere a patterned requirement for marriage. For the purpose of my argument the procurement of heads and virilities should be for *the magic acquisition of fertility as a substance,* though this meaning cannot always be ruled out as a motive, nor can simple proof of masculine prowess.

Although collecting fertility in dangerous circumstances in Indonesia and elsewhere is doubtless a manly activity, not all men could be successful at it, and its requirement for marriage was not everywhere absolute. Still, the collecting of masculinity was at least something of a male responsibility and social desideratum. In the western islands of the Torres Straits, "in olden days the war dance, which was performed after a successful foray, would be the most powerful excitant to a marriageable girl, especially if a young man had distinguished himself sufficiently to bring home the head of someone he had killed."[18] Haddon was told that "this was one of the chief reasons for head-hunting in the past, as it still is adduced on the neighboring mainland of New Guinea."[19]

The Dyak often told Gomes, "the young men are so anxious to bring home a human head...because the women have so decided a preference for a man who has been able to give proof of his bravery by killing one of the enemy."[20] Among the Vonum (aboriginals of

Taiwan), a man "who has refrained from head-hunting can obtain a wife among the less attractive girls, but a savage belle would look for a husband among the young braves who had proven their valour and intrepidity."[21]

The suspicion lingers, however, that the acquired magic virility of the head hunter is the real issue, the actual getting of the head itself, not prowess as such. In the *locus classicus* of headhunting among the Dyak of Borneo, "He who succeeded in bringing back a head, no matter how obtained, was immediately received as a distinguished member of the community and had a free choice of all the girls of his village."[22] Since the head per se (or, perhaps more precisely, the brain) was the critical matter, the heads of women or even of children might be taken also among Indonesian headhunters. Similarly, in Nubia, "whether the killing was done in fair fight [or] in the form of murder did not matter,"[23] which hardly argues prowess as the main concern: "The rules of hospitality were very strictly and conscientiously observed, but a guest, after he had left the house, was often waylaid and his throat cut, thus enabling his host to enter as a fully qualified murderer the honourable state of matrimony."[24] Among the Dyak, the Alfurs of Ceram, or Minahassa, and of Sumatra, emphasis was placed on the necessity of head-taking before marriage.[25] But "exception has been taken by some writers to the statement as being too absolute, although they admit that it would be exceedingly difficult for a man to obtain a wife unless he were provided with the required trophy."[26] Perhaps in headhunting, as in all other cultural ideals, the rules must be tempered for the failures in life.

A further motive for headhunting is found among the Kuki of Assam, who believe (somewhat like the Celts) that "all the enemies whom a man has killed will be in attendance on him as slaves" — in the Kuki case in an afterlife.[27] And some Indonesians believe an enemy whose head has been taken will be transformed into a guardian spirit.[28] A Kayan chief in Borneo said of headhunting, "It brings us blessings, plentiful harvests, and keeps off sickness and pains; those who were once our enemies, hereby become our guardians, our friends, our benefactors."[29] The reasoning seems strange, and yet the belief is very old in Europe, in Asia, and in both Americas. Its very strangeness argues a common antiquity.

An additional nuance in Indonesian headhunding is contributed by the Toradja of Celebes. Among them, headhunting was thought necessary to provide spirit-food for the ancestors. When headhunting was suppressed, "there was an intense anxiety lest the ancestral spirits, no longer fed with a 'harvest' of enemy heads, would perforce eat the villagers themselves."[30] Another interesting fact is that the long-mysterious degenerative disease (in the central nervous system) called *kuru* among the Fore of montane New Guinea was specifically the result of eating insufficiently cooked human brains.[31]

The practice of headhunting extended aboriginally from mainland southeastern Asia and the Indonesian islands (Sumatra, Borneo, Ceram, Celebes, etc., to Taiwan and the Philippines) eastward and southward to Melanesia and New Guinea.[32] In New Guinea (as in a moment we shall see), the sexual "facts of life" take a dramatic turn. But first we must allude to the curious species-specific neoteny of the human animal, its prolonged childhood and long-delayed sexual maturation.

Headhunting for the acquisition of male fertility is in many parts of the world based on a very old assumption regarding puberty that masculinity is a commodity that *must be obtained from other males*. Hormonally, indeed, the female is the "norm" for the human species; and it requires special androgens, active from the early embryo onward, to change the undifferentiated *Anlage* of the fetus into a male individual. Something like this also occurs psychologically, in the long-delayed change from a boy-child into a man: women can make babies, but only men can make a boy into a man.[33] Genetically, of course, this is done by the Y chromosome already contributed by the male parent's spermatozoan at the moment of conception; *viz.*

maleness is a male contribution. Nevertheless, there is still much to be done *psychologically* by the father and other male surrogates, during the growth of the boy into the approved pattern of manhood in each society.

As a consequence, almost worldwide, there are magic male rituals — we even have evidence of puberty rituals in the Old Stone Age (e.g., at Montespan) — that are typically patterned on ordinary birth but zealously kept secret from women who do not understand these male mysteries.[34] Puberty rites are a *rebirth* of the initiate from the male group, and not uncommonly with a significant surgical editing specifically of the genitals. The ancient notion that *external forces* must be brought to bear to make boys into men is at best true only psychologically. As to physical traits, the notion is actually based on *ignorance* of the facts of life regarding puberty, a transformation that comes from the *automatic* unfolding of an inner entelechy, under the influence of male hormones in adolescence. It is the universal *species-specific neoteny* of the human animal, the long delay of sexual maturity, and the endocrine facts of masculinity that make such a dramatic contrast between child and adult male and thus propose the rationale for these worldwide rituals.[35] It is true that a male Y chromosome is needed to engender a male; and it can come only from a male. And it is true that males are necessary as a social model for manhood in any society. But physical virility and sexual potency are not the product of any ritual, however gruesome.

The ancient concept of maleness as a finitely limited substance that must be taken from others is well developed among the Asmat of Papua, an almost untouched tribe who were cannibals and head-hunters until about 1954. But cannibalism was not the chief end of their headhunting, only a secondary adjunct to it: the getting of virility and of fertility are the real goals. To this end, the brains of enemy victims are eaten by the old men, soon to be ritual ancestor-spirits, and the decorated head of the enemy victim is placed in the groin of the adolescent initiate, soon to become a man. "For a considerable time the skull must rest between the thighs of the initiate, almost touching his genitals; thus there is thought to be a relationship between the skull and the genitals of the youngster, whose initiation marks his entry into manhood."[36] The initiate not only absorbs the vitality of the headhunted victim but also takes on his name. In the Asmat origin myth of headhunting, the decapitated head can speak (as in the Orpheus legend of the Gaulish, Welsh, and Irish Celts) and hence can give his name.

As so commonly, worldwide, this *rite de passage* is symbolized "with a ritual death and ritual rebirth. A cosmic event — the daily course of the sun — seems to have suggested the ritual: a parallel in which sunrise is thought of as birth and sunset as death" — which forcibly recalls the metaphor of the Ofnet skulls.[37] "There appears to be a definite association between headhunting and cosmic events . . . Headhunting is required for the bodily development of young men and for their sexual maturation ["head," *wé-áhe,* means literally "fruit of man," the tree being the human body] . . . There is also a vague relationship between headhunting and sexual inter-course" — although taking a head himself is not specifically required of a young man before his marriage.[38] Fruit-eating birds and flying animals are equated with headhunters in the rich iconography of Asmat woodcarvers. To these Papuan cannibals, the sago tree, their staple food, represents a human being. But eating sago or a fruit "head" is not mere inference for brain – seed eating. In one major ritual, the sago tree represents a woman, into the center of which are introduced, like semen, the larvae of the capricorn beetle; and "the ritual cutting down such a tree incorporates many references to headhunting," according to the Dutch ethnographer Gerbrands.[39] Especially significant in the ritual symbolism is the *an* tray, woven of the topmost fronds of the sago palm.

In former days the *an* was used to collect the brains of a headhunted enemy. With the pointed end of a stone ax a hole was made in the temple of a freshly-cleaned skull. The brains were removed from the skull with a bamboo spatula, and collected in the *an*. The *an* filled with brains must have resembled amazingly the *an* filled with sago worms. In this connection it should be noted that the *an* is identified with the vagina in Asmat culture. Brains and grubs have a strong fertility aspect, and... the grubs are identified with sperm... The brains of a headhunted enemy carry along strong implications of fertility. The fertility concept underlies headhunting in general... The decorated head was then laid between the spread legs of the initiate or placed against his groin.; There the head had to remain for two or three days.[40]

After this, a ceremonial canoe-trip downriver and on the sea to the west, toward the *safan* land of the ancestors, was made with the initiate, during which he acted like an old man; but on returning eastward (upriver) toward the sunrise, he was like a child who had everything to learn of life. The prow of the canoe, called the "penis," was almost always decorated with elaborate woodcarving. Also intricately carved is the *bis*, or ancestor-pole set up at each fireplace in the *yeu*, or men's house which is divided into an upriver and a downriver portion.

Asmat symbolism is unusually complete, as delineated by the Rev. Zegwaard, the Dutch art historian and ethnographer Adrian Gerbrands, and the many art objects collected by the late Michael Rockefeller. For the Asmat, brains and sago grubs and sperm are ritually identical; the head of an enemy promotes adolescent fertility; tree = person has a head = fruit; the tree-woman is inseminated with semen-grubs = enemy brains, both eaten to promote fertility; the upriver and downriver intermarrying kingroups reciprocally collect grubs – brains – semen for one another; the life-journey and the sun's have an up and downriver east – west axis; an ancestor-pole is at each fireplace — and, to complete the cycle, the used ancestor-poles (of which the à-jour-carved pennant is "penis" like the canoe prow) in the men's house (where the youth is now a full member) were taken into the jungle, there to promote with their fertility-power the growth of the sago, one of which is ritually inseminated with brains – sago worms placed in the *an* tray – womb. (Some of the carved wooden food bowls have a male and a female handle-figure at opposite ends, signifying coitus, with the sago worms – brains – semen in the central womb between, quite like the *an* tray made of sago fronds and the semen – grubs – brains when they have matured after being placed in the sago – tree – woman.

Like the tribes of the coast of Papua made virtually inaccessible by vast mangrove swamps — hence these deeply rooted native customs cannot have been a rapid post-colonial diffusion — the natives of montane New Guinea have been almost totally unkown until the last half-century (as indeed were the remote tribes of the China – India "Hump" region). Yet they too already give evidence of the magic making of manhood, here with actual male substance. The Australian ethnologist F. E. Williams (discoverer of the "Vailala Madness") has reported striking facts concerning the puberty rituals of tribes of the Trans-Fly.[41] Here there is institutionalized sodomy as an integral part of the initiation of youths, in which the adolescents are symbolically treated as women until they are sufficiently inseminated by their adult male initiators and thereby made into men. A parallel case, though performed in a differing manner, is found in another Papuan group. The psychiatrist Stoller and the anthropologist Herdt summarize the Sambia attitude:

Since maleness (as opposed to the mere possession of male genitals) is not natural or innate, and since the male body is felt to lack an endogenous mechanism for creating semen — the basis of masculine development — it follows that men regard constant insemination (which they compare to breast feeding) as the only means for boys to grow, mature, and attain manly competence. Hence, starting with first-stage initiation, fellation — to be indulged in as often as possible — is fully institutionalized. (Semen, in this respect, functions analogously to the artificial intake of androgens in a eunuch). This behavior is a tremendous secret that must be kept, under pain of death, from all children and females.[42]

Both the Keraki and the Sambia rationales are related to another notion of New Guinea natives, earlier reported by Margaret Mead, equating milk and semen.[43] Among the Arapesh, parent – child nurturance is polarized, rather than male–female gender differences. Males are merely specialized for prenatal nurturance of offspring and females are postnatal (thus, when he becomes a father, a man is commiserated on all the exhausting hard work he has performed). A young man must even "grow" his fiancée by bringing food to her, and premarital intercourse is forbidden not so much for reasons of any Oceanic Puritanism as that the use of semen in growth and in procreation are diametrically opposed. Premature coitus stunts growth. One must achieve his own growth first, before growing babies.

Among the Sambia, as among many tribes of montane New Guinea, masculinity and femininity are rigorously polarized, often with cruel conflict between the sexes.

Beyond this [polarization] is the conviction that women deplete men of their strength and eventually of life itself by robbing—emptying—them, through sexual intercourse, of their male substance, semen. For men, semen is literally the stuff of existence, of vitality, and the sole origin of the anatomy identified as maleness. Yet it is also needed by women to strengthen themselves, so that they can produce breast milk, and can create and form babies. Boys cannot become men without a steady supply of exogenous semen, for, men believe, the male body cannot manufacture semen. But women want it too, and their needs and demands are endless.

Women pollute and deplete: two strains that threaten masculinity and forever intrude into marriage. Examples: men are uneasy about what they eat, particulary their wives' food; they fear intimacy; inexplicable illness and failure in hunting can be blamed on one's wife; sexual relationships are often poisoned with suspiciousness, covetousness, and expectations of adultery. And yet, out of this morass of hostility and silence, demands and punishments, squabbles and curses, wife-beating, murder, and female suicides, family units are created. For there is also, between the sexes, need and gratification, respect, sharing and pleasure in children. And the children are party to—objects, audiences, loved ones, and pawns—these dramas.[44]

Girls mature spontaneously from self-activating blood; "femaleness is a natural development... but maleness is not natural; it is, rather, a personal achievement, a power that boys and men seize only through the initiations of their ritual cult.... Men regard attaining adult reproductive competence as far less certain for males than females.[45]

Given these ideas, curiously, among the Keraki "a homosexual stage is considered essential to the attainment of psychosexual maturity," through ritual initiatory sodomy,[46] and the Sambia have no less than six rites, including prolonged fellation, to produce and lead into full manhood, with marriage and fatherhood. Similar patterns are well known elsewhere in New Guinea.[47] Sambia fellation is rigidly structured by "incest" rules that prevent sexual contacts with kinsmen, so that only the bachelors among alien groups may be the provendors.

At puberty and its third-stage initiation, adolescent youths become the dominant suppliers of semen for a new group of initiates. During this time, all contacts with females are prohibited, and the strongest social pressures are brought to bear on boys so that they will conform. This results in a precise, rigid structure of ritualized masculinity.... Later, with marriage and a family, all homosexual activity is to end. Men thereafter act exclusively as heterosexual adults... and though heterosexually severely suppressed, boys are encouraged by their fathers and elders to acquire semen so that they, too, can achieve marriage and fatherhood. The function of the ritual cult is to create a powerful, dependable warrior's masculinity, with its very precisely tuned mode of heterosexuality.[48]

The practice is thus both required and codified. For an adult male to fantasy active fellation of a prepubescent boy "would be perversion — shocking. It would be, in our terms, homosexuality."[49]

Notes

1. In Burma: John Butler, *Travels and Adventures in the Province of Assam* (London: Smith, Elder, 1855); B. S. Carey and H. N. Tuck, *The Chin Hills*, 2 vols. (Rangoon, Burma: Superintendent of Government Printing, 1896); P. R. T. Gurdon, *The Khasis* (London: Macmillan, 1914); Ola Hanson, *The*

Kachins, Their Customs and Practices (Rangoon, Burma: American Baptist Mission Press, 1913); T. C. Hodson, Naga Tribes of Manipur (London: Macmillan, 1911); Hodson, The Meitheis (London: Nutt, 1908); J. H. Hutton, The Angami Nagas (London: Macmillan, 1921); Hutton, The Sema Nagas (London: Macmillan, 1921); John Macrae, "Account of the Kookies," in Asiatick Researches, vol. 7 (Calcutta, 1831); J. P. Mills, The Ao Nagas (London: Macmillan, 1926); Mills, The Lhota Nagas (London: Macmillan, 1922); A Playfair, The Garos (London: Nutt, 1909); J. G. Scott and J. P. Hardiman, Gazetteer of Upper Burma and the Shan States, 5 vols. (Rangoon: Superintendent of Public Printing, 1900 – 1901); J. Shakespear, The Lushei Kuki Clans (London: Macmillan, 1912); Shakespear, History of Upper Assam, Upper Burmah and Northeastern Frontier (London: Macmillan, 1914); William Carlson Smith, The Ao Naga Tribe of Assam (London: Macmillan, 1925). For general surveys, see Carl A. Schmitz, Kopfjäger und Kannibalen (Basel: Museum für Völkerkunde and Schweizerisches Museum für Volkskunde, 1961) and Meinhard Schuster, "Kopfjagd in Indonesien," Ph.D. diss., J.W. Goethe University, Frankfurt, 1960.

In Indonesia: A. S. Bickmore, Travels in the East Indian Archipelago (London: Murray, 1868); J. W. Davidson, The Island of Formosa (London and New York: Macmillan, 1903); W. Müller, "Uber die Wildenstämme der Insel Formosa," Zeitschrift für Ethnologie 1910, 42:241; G. A. Wilken, Het Animisme bij de volken van den Indischen Archipel (Amsterdam: H. de Bussy, 1884), p. 124; C. Wilkes, Narrative of the United States Exploring Expedition During the Years 1838 – 1842, 5 vols. (Philadelphia and London: Lea and Blanchard, 1845), 5:363; D. C. Worcester, The Philippine Islands and Their People (New York: Macmillan, 1898); Worcester, "The Non-Christian Tribes of Northern Luzon," Philippine Journal of Science, 1:439. See also Teuku Jacob, "The Problem of Head-Hunting and Brain-Eating Among Pleistocene Men in Indonesia," Archaeology and Physical Anthropology in Oceania, (1972), 7(2):81 – 91.

2. Gerald D. Berreman, "Peoples and Cultures of the Himalayas," Asian Survey (June 1963), 3(6):289 – 312; Smith, Ao Naga, pp. 68 – 71.

3. J. H. Hutton, "The Significance of Head-Hunting in Assam," (1928) 403; T. C. Hodson, "Head-Hunting Among the Hill Tribes of Assam," Folk-Lore [London] (1909), 20:141.

4. R. B. Onians, The Origins of European Thought (New York: Arno Press, 1973), p. 127 n. 2.

5. Spenser B. St. John, Life in the Forests of the Far East, 2 vols. (London: Smith, Elder, 1862), 1:204.

6. J. D. Freeman, "Severed Heads That Germinate," *Psychoanalysis and the Interpretation of Symbolic Behaviour*, Section 25 (June 23, 1975), Symposium, Australian and New Zealand Association for the Advancement of Science Congress. See also Freeman, "Thunder, Blood, and the Nicknaming of God's Creatures," *ibid*, 1965.

7. V. Gordon Childe, *What Happened in History* (Baltimore: Penguin Books, 1942), p. 16, citing W. H. R. Rivers.

8. D. Prain, "The Angami Nagas," *Revue coloniale internationale* [Amsterdam] (1887), 5:492, in Edward Westermarck, *The History of Human Marriage*, 5th ed., 3 vols.; (London: Macmillan, 1925), 2:3.

9. Westermarck, *History of Human Marriage*, 1:52, citing J. W. Davidson, *The Island of Formosa* [Taiwan], p. 566; D. C. Worcester, *Philippine Islands*, p. 439; A. S. Bickmore, *Travels*, p. 205; E. H. Gomes, *Seventeen Years Among the Sea Dyaks of Borneo* (London: Seeley, 1911), p. 74; see also pp. 73, 87; E. T. Dalton, *The Descriptive Ethnology of Bengal* (Calcutta: Office of the Superintendent of Government Printing, 1872), p. 40; T. C. Hodson, "Head-Hunting," p. 141.

10. Westermarck, *History of Human Marriage*, 1:52, citing Hodson, "Head-Hunting," p. 141.

11. J. L. Krapf, *Reisen in Ost-Afrika*, 2 vols. (Kornthal and Stuttgart: F. A. Brockhaus, 1908), 1:274. Strabo (*Geographica* 15.2.14) wrote that the ancient Karmanians were considered marriagable only after they had killed an enemy; the Masai, of the Nilotic Sudan, only after going on several raids. A. C. Hollis, *The Masai; Their Language and Folklore* (Oxford: Clarendon Press, 1905), p. 302 n 1.

12. T. Waitz, *Anthropologie der Naturvölker*, 6 vols. (Leipzig: Fleischer, 1859–1872), 2:502, 515; C. E. X. d'Héricourt, *Voyage sur la côte orientale de la Mer Rouge, dans le pays d'Adel et le royaume de Choa* (Paris: Bertrand, 1841), pp. 241, 245, 313; James Bruce of Kinnaird, *Travels to Discover the Source of the Nile*, 5 vols. (Edinburgh: Robinson, 1790), 3:346; G. A. Haggenmacher, "Reise in Somaliland," in *Petermann's Mittheilungen* (1876) 10, Erganzungsheft no. 47, p. 29; A. E. Brehm, *Reiseskizzen aus Nord-Ost-Afrika*, 3 parts (Jena: Mauke, 1855), 2:234; Ismail Ibn Ali Abu'l Fedah, *La géographie d'Aboulféda*, M. Reinaud, trans., 2 vols. (Paris: Imprimerie nationale, 1848–1883), 1:210; Muhammad ibn 'Abd Allah Ibn Batutah, *Voyages*, S. Lee, trans. (London: Oriental Translation Fund, 1829), p. 7; Adjà Ibn al-Hind, *Les merveilles de l'Inde*, M. L. Devic, trans. (Paris, 1878), pp. 97ff.

13. J. N. Demeunier, *L'esprit des usages et des coutumes des différents peuples*, 2 vols. (Paris: Pissot, 1736), 2:47.

14. Waitz-Gerland, *Anthropologie* (1872), 6:576, 648; G. Landtman, "The Magic of the Kiwai Papuans in Warfare," *Journal of the Royal Anthropological Institute* (1916), 36:324.

15. F. Cailliaud, *Voyage à Meroë, au Fleuve Blanc, au-delà de Fazoql*, 4 vols. (Paris: Imprimerie royale, 1826 – 1827), 3:32; Julius Braun, *Naturgeschichte der Sage* (Munich: Bruckmann, 1864 – 1865), 1:49; 2 Samuel 3:14.

16. F. Liebrecht, *Zur Volkskunde* (Heilbronn: Henninger, 1879), p. 94.

17. Gualterius Mapes, *De Nugis Curalium* (London: Camden Society, 1850), p. 79.

18. Westermarck, *History of Human Marriage*, 2:2, citing Haddon.

19. A. C. Haddon, *Reports of the Cambridge Anthropological Expedition to Torres Straits*, 6 vols. (New York: Johnson Reprint, 1971) 5:222 [originally 1901 – 1935; vol. 5, 1904].

20. Gomes, *Seventeen Years*, p. 73; Westermarck, *History of Human Marriage*, 2:2; see also C. A. Bock, *The Head-Hunters of Borneo* (London: Low, Marston, Searle & Rivington, 1881), p. 216.

21. Davidson, *Island of Formosa*, p. 569; see also W. Müller, "Wildenstämme," p. 241.

22. E. A. Francis, "Westkust van Borneo," *Tijdskrift voor Nederlandsch Indie* [Batavia], (1842), 4, pt. 2, pp. 10ff; cf. Smith, *Ao Naga*, pp. 68 – 71.

23. J. W. Sager, "Notes on the History, Religion and Customs of the Nuba," *Sudan Notes and Records* [Khartoum], (1922), 5:155.

24. Robert Briffault, *The Mothers*, 3 vols. (London: George Allen & Unwin, New York: Macmillan, 1927; New York: Johnson Reprint Corporation, 1969), 2:185.

25. M. T. H. Perelaer, *Ethnographische beschrijving des Dajaks* (Zal t-Bommel: Noman, 1870), pp. 48, 171; Bock, *The Head-Hunters of Borneo*; Bock, *Een Reis in Oost en Zuid-Borneo, van Koetoi naar Hanjermassin* (The Hague: Nidhoff, 1881), pp. 92, 97; S.W. Tromp, "En reis naar de bovenlanden van Koetei," *Tijdschrift voor Indische Taal-, Land- en Volkenkunde* (1876), 23:295; H. von Dewall, "Aanterkenigen omtrent de nordoostkuste van Borneo," ibid. (1855), 4:450; A. van Ekris, "Iets over Ceram en de Alfoeren," *Bijdragen tot de taal-, land- en volkenkunde van Nederlandsch-Indie*, N. V. (1857), 1:82; N. Graafland, *De Minakassa: Haar verleden en haar Tegenvoordige Toestand*, 2 vols. (Rotterdam: Wijt & Zonen, 1867 – 1869), 1:317; P. J. Veth, "Het landschap Aboeng en de Aboengers op Sumatra," *Tijdschrift van het Koniglik Nederlandsch Aardrijkikskundig Genootschap* (1887), 3:45ff; C. M. Pleyte, "De geographische Verbreiding van het Koppensnellen in der Oost Indischen Archipel," ibid. (1891), 8:908ff.

26. Briffault, *The Mothers*, 2:185 n. 6. "But it appears that the condition was originally absolutely indispensable," 2:186, citing C. A. L. M. Schwaner, *Borneo: Beschrijving van het Stroomgebied van den Barito* (Amsterdam: van Kampen, 1853 – 1854), 1:191; S. Müller, *Reizen en Onderzoekingen in den Indischen Archipel* (Amsterdam: Müller, 1857), 1:253; F. J. P. Sachse, *Het Eiland Seram en sijne Bewoners* (Leiden: Brill, 1907), p. 209—although the practice had largely been put down by the Dutch (see P. J. Veth, *Borneo's Wester-afdeeling*, 2 vols. (Zaltbommel: Noman en Zoon, 1854 – 1856), 2:277ff.

27. E. T. Dalton, *Descriptive Ethnology of Bengal* (Calcutta: Office of the Superintendent of Government Printing, 1872), p. 46.

28. H. Ling Roth, *The Natives of Sarawak and British North Borneo*, 2 vols. (London: Truslove & Hanson, 1896), 2:141; A. C. Haddon, *Head-Hunters, Black, White and Brown* (London: Methuen, 1901), p. 394.

29. W. H. Furness, *The Home-Life of Borneo Head-Hunters* (Philadelphia: Lippincott, 1902), p. 59.

30. Weston La Barre, *The Ghost Dance: Origins of Religion* (New York: Doubleday, 1970), p. 306.

31. D. C. Gajdusek and V. Zigas, "Kuru: Clinical, Pathological and Epidemiological Study of an Acute Progressive Degenerative Disease of the Central Nervous System among Natives of the Eastern Highlands of New Guinea," *American Journal of Medicine*, (1959), 26:442 – 469; D. C. Gajdusek and Michael Alpers, "Definitive Bibliography on Kuru in New Guinea," (ms. 1966); see also John D. Matthews, Robert Glasse, and Shirley Lindenbaum, "Kuru and Cannibalism," *Lancet*, August 24, 1968, pp. 449–52.

32. For Melanesia: George Brown, *Melanesians and Polynesians* (London: Macmillan, 1910); R. H. Codrington, *The Melanesians* (Oxford: Clarendon Press, 1969); Haddon, *Head-Hunters*; Haddon, *Reports*; Albert B. Lewis, *Ethnology of Melanesia*, part 5, (Chicago: Field Museum of Natural History, 1926); Alfred Penny, *Ten Years in Melanesia* (London: Gardner, Darton, 1887); W. H. R. Rivers, *The History of Melanesian Society*, 2 vols. (Cambridge: Cambridge University Press, 1914); H. H. Romilly, *The Western Pacific and New Guinea* (London: Murray, 1887); Erhard Schlesier, *Die Melanesische Geheimkulte* (Göttingen: Musterschmidt, 1958); C. R. H. Taylor, *A Pacific Bibliography: Printed Matter Relating to the Native Peoples of Polynesia, Melanesia and Micronesia* Polynesian Society Memoir no. 24, (Wellington, New Zealand, 1951); R. Thurnwald, "Ethno-psychologische

Studien an Südseevölkern," *Zeitschrift für angewandenet Psychologie*, supplement 6, 1913.

For New Guinea: Brown, *Melanesians and Polynesians;* Haddon, *Head-Hunters;* Haddon, *Reports;* Romilly, *Western Pacific;* Taylor, *Pacific Bibliography;* Thurnwald, "Ethno-psychologische Studien."

33. La Barre, *Ghost Dance*, ch. 3, "The First World," pp. 93 – 115.

34. La Barre, *Ghost Dance*, pp. 158, 390, 396 – 98, 412.

35. La Barre, *The Human Animal* (Chicago: University of Chicago Press, 1954), pp. 303 – 34.

36. G. A. Zegwaard, "Headhunting Practices of the Asmat of Netherlands New Guinea," *American Anthropologist* (1959), 61:1020 – 41, p. 1027.

37. Zegwaard, "Headhunting Practices," p. 1027.

38. Zegwaard, "Headhunting Practices," pp. 1037, 1039, 1041.

39. Adrian A. Gerbrands, "Art and Artist in Asmat Society," in Michael C. Rockefeller, *The Asmat of New Guinea*, pp. 11 – 39 (New York: Museum of Primitive Art, 1962), p. 17. The Asmat were headhunters and cannibals until about 1954, when the Dutch reestablished a government patrol post among them.

40. Gerbrands, *Art and Artist*, p. 18; cf. pp. 32, 38 – 39. For ancestor figures with heads held in front of the genitals, see Rockefeller, *Asmat*, pp. 270 – 73, 278C, 309B, 310 – 11 AB, and 314; for bowl and tray figures *in coitu*, pp. 290, 294.

41. F. E. Williams, *Papuans of the Trans-Fly* (Oxford: Clarendon Press, 1956); see also G. Osterwal, "The Position of the Bachelor in the Upper Tor Territory," *American Anthropologist* (1959), 61:829 – 38.

42. Robert J. Stoller and Gilbert H. Herdt, "The Development of Masculinity: A Cross-Cultural Contribution," *Journal of the American Psychoanalytic Association* (1982), 30:29 – 59, p. 42.

43. Margaret Mead, *Sex and Temperament in Three Primitive Societies* (New York: Morrow, 1935). "Among the Mohave Indians it is a standard cultural belief that after the sixth lunar month of pregnancy the fetus in the uterus ingests *orally* and feeds on the semen deposited in the pregnant woman's vagina by her sexual partner." George Devereux, "Mohave Pregnancy," *Acta Americana* (1948), 6:89 – 116; see also Devereux, "The Voices of Children," in *Basic Problems of Ethnopsychiatry*, pp. 105 – 21 (Chicago: University of Chicago Press, 1980), p. 115.

44. Stoller and Herdt, "Development of Masculinity," pp. 38 – 39.

45. Stoller and Herdt, "Development of Masculinity," p. 41.

46. Georgene Seward, *Sex and the Social Order* (New York: McGraw-Hill, 1946), citing Ruth Benedict, "Sex in Primitive Society," *American Journal of Orthopsychiatry* (1939), 9:570–74.

47. M. R. Allen, *Male Cults and Secret Initiation in Melanesia* (Melbourne: Melbourne University Press, 1967). See also Paula Brown and Georgeda Buchbinder, eds., *Man and Woman in the New Guinea Highlands* (Washington: Special Publication no. 8, American Anthropological Association, 1976); L. L. Langness, "Sexual Antagonism in the New Guinea Highlands: A Bena Bena Example," *Oceania*, (1967), 37:161 – 77; Langness, "Ritual Power and Male Domination in the New Guinea Highlands," *Ethos* (1974), 2:189 – 212; M. J. Meggitt, "Male-Female Relationships in the Highlands of Australian New Guinea," *American Anthropologist* (1964), vol. 66, part 2, pp. 204 – 24; R. F. Salisbury, "The Siane of the Eastern Highlands," in P. Lawrence and M. Meggitt, eds., *Gods, Ghosts and Men in Melanesia*, pp. 50 – 57 (Melbourne: Melbourne University Press, 1965).

48. Stoller and Herdt, "Development of Masculinity," pp. 42, 43, 44.

49. Stoller and Herdt, "Development of Masculinity," p. 42 n. 10.

CHAPTER III

Ethnographic: New World

American Indians also had the belief that manhood is not the result of growth promoted by internal factors but must be expropriated from supernatural sources outside. Therefore, about the time of puberty, the Indian youth sought "medicine power" in a lonely vigil in a remote place. The "vision quest" was for medicine power from *manitou* (Algonquian), *wakan* (Siouan), *orenda* (Iroquoian), etc., a kind of *mana* lurking in impersonal cosmic or wild animal sources.[1] In South America the emphasis was on seeking shamanic power, but elsewhere the vision quest was made by all males — evidence for which is found even among the advanced societies of Middle America.[2]

Exactly as food must be found in the life-giving flesh of hunted animals (or of plants), so also must spiritual-, soul-, or generative-power be sought from outside.[3] The logic is crystal clear. In hunting, life is expropriated from outside; to engender life, male potency must be expropriated from outside. In this "expropriative theory of puberty," precisely from the vision quest (spirit-hunt) comes

that potency and power that each man needs to become a man, and if the process goes awry, he remains the not-man *berdache*, frozen in a frightened pre-masculine childhood. This power is the "medicine" of each man, most especially of the shaman; and in Amazonia this power raises shamans to the status of living gods. The power concept is a native rationale of the "facts of life," of puberty, male potency and procreativity.[4]

Even the gods, in the more complex agricultural societies, must be fed souls for their well-being and continued existence. Indeed, the whole purpose of Aztec warfare was the acquisition of enemy soul-power in unremitting warfare, and to that end "more victims were sacrificed annually to the god Xipe than died a natural death in all Mexico; Cortez saw 136,000 skulls deposited in the great temple; Prescott estimated a yearly total of 20,000−40,000 human sacrifices in all Mexico; and at the dedication in 1486 of a new temple, 70,000 prisoners of war, collected for this purpose over some years, were sacrificed to the god Huitzilopochtli."[5]

Copious iconographic and archeological data, in fact, are forcing a reexamination of human head-taking in all of ancient Mesoamerica. "Decapitation, from all evidence, seems to have been an integral part of indigenous ceremonial life, warfare, and personal achievement from a considerably early era and throughout most of Mexico and Central America."[6] Human headhunting in war is recorded for the Acaxee, Cora, Tarahumara, Yaqui, Tepahue, Sinaloa, Tepehuane, Xixime, Huastecan, Nicaro, and Zapotec, reaching a peak among the Aztec of Tenochtitlán in the temple collections. In Oaxaca there was a fashion of wearing human heads upside-down as part of a necklace, and

shrunken heads were displayed or worn as part of the garments or vestments of important personages, especially among the Zapotecs of Oaxaca and the southern Mayas. Trophy heads were avidly taken in battle, especially by the Huastecans and the people of the West Coast... ritual decapitation, the taking of trophy heads, severed heads, and ceremonial cannibalism constituted a far more important and pan-Mesoamerican trait than was previously recognized.[7]

Decapitation was associated with numerous earth-fertility goddesses, and with the ritual alcoholic drink pulque and the maguey plant. There was "strong conceptualism linking agriculture, fertility, birth, and the [ritual] ballgame with severed heads and decapitation [as well as with female and] male agro-fertility deities."[8] The impressively pan-Mesoamerican distribution, indeed through many archeological periods, raises "the possibility that human decapitation developed... as a trait of the Paleolithic Old World culture and may have been carried into the American hemisphere as a trait of the Archaic substratum that underlies Mesoamerican cultures."[9] Certainly the very old Bone Cult of Eurasiatic hunters remains visible in the essentially Late Paleolithic and Mesolithic basic cultures of the American Indians, coming from Siberia some tens of thousands of years ago. The eminent European Americanist Åke Hultkrantz writes that

The oldest stratum of religion, then, is represented by the conceptualizations and rites of the hunters (and of the fishers and gatherers).... It is important that the felled prey be ritually [placed] with their bones arranged according to the structure of the living body, as only in this way may the return of the animal be assured.... This animal ceremonialism is at times addressed not to the spirit of the animal but to the master of animals of the animal species.[10]

Since the Americas are culturally something of a "Mesolithic fossil" of the Old World, both the bone cult and the "master of animals" were universal in the New World.

It is not surprising, therefore, to find the old Eurasiatic concept of *muelos* also prevalent among American Indians. It is recently reported by Anne Straus for the Northern Cheyenne that "the final locus of the life principle is the marrow-filled bones of the skeleton after the flesh has fallen away"[11] — a belief probably representative of all American Indians, North and South. A Rockefeller-financed expedition to the Kiowa led by the late Alexander Lesser discovered in this Plains tribe the belief that the bones of any animal, including humans, were the contribution of the male parent, again a concept probably universal among American Indians (Lowie, for example, recorded an Assiniboine story of a woman who made love with her husband's sister, who subsequently bore a child, but of course it was boneless because it lacked a male parent).[12] Bone marrow is thus the source not only of male seed but also of male-given bones themselves.

In the voluminous materials of Onians, hair on the head and hair appearing at puberty (on jaw or pubes) are belived to be so located because of their proximity to the main storage place and conduit of the *muelos*.[13] Like male animal horns, hair is the sign and the locus of virility and strength. Samson's great strength lay in his hair; folklore is full of such beliefs — and "sperm" whales are so called because of the large quantities of spermaceti in the huge tuns of their skulls. Short of the collecting of heads, then, the collecting of scalp trophies may serve as emblems of male prowess and power in war. Taking of the scalp was ancient European and protohistoric Scythian. The chief in the Mongolian – Hun permafrost burial at Pazyryk in Siberia had been scalped. Scalping was also sporadic in Siberia in ethnographic times (Ostyak, Samoyed, and Vogul).[14]

It is now recognized that scalping and head-taking are aspects, alternative or mutually exclusive, of the same larger complex that is intercontinental in scope. The *locus classicus* of American Indian headhunting is of course Amazonia, but it probably extends northward through the little-known tribes of isthmian Middle America to the Aztec god-feeders and the cannibals of northern Mexico and coastal Texas. In North America the *locus classicus* of scalping extends from the mouth of the St. Lawrence to the Gulf of Mexico, mostly east of the Mississippi, especially among Muskhogeans and Iroquoians.[15] However, there are sporadic enclaves of the unexpected in both continents. Scalping reappears in the Gran Chaco and part of the Guianas in South America, whereas the whole head is taken by the Makah of the Northwest.[16] Indeed, the notorious "shrunken heads" made by the Jívaro do not include the skull and are really only very generous "scalps" that include neck and even shoulder skin to allow for slow shrinkage, in a process that is sufficiently familiar.[17] Indeed, among the Aztec, the priest impersonating the god

Xipe dressed in the entire skin of the sacrificial victim.[18] Again, I do not contemplate here a comprehensive study of American Indian scalping – headhunting, but only a sketch of representative samples. The Jívaro Indians of the dense tropical rain forest of Andean Ecuador "have long been famous for their warlike practices, but the assumptions about reality upon which they predicate such behavior have not been systematically studied and analyzed.... Among these concepts has recently been discovered a deep-seated belief that killing leads to the acquisition of souls which provide a supernatural power conferring immunity from death."[19] The Jívaro lived in scattered nuclear-family houses in very loose neighborhood groupings. As they are constantly making war raids, so also they constantly fear them. The Jívaro have the universal Indian vision-quest – they seek the *arutam-* (vision, apparition) *wakanI* (spirit) as "security from the ever-felt menace of death" — but with the understandable modification that the young boy has his father along to protect him.

A person is not born with an arutam soul. Such a soul must be acquired, and in certain traditional ways. The acquisition of this type of soul is considered to be so important to an adult male's survival that a boy's parents do not expect him to live past puberty without one.... A boy begins seeking an arutam soul about the age of six years. Accompanied most commonly by his father, he makes a pilgrimage to the sacred waterfall of his neighborhood. This is always the highest waterfall within a few days travel. It is believed to be the rendezvous of these souls which wander about as breezes, scattering the spray of the long cascade. By night the pilgrims sleep near the falls in a simple lean-to. Here they fast, drink tobacco water, and await the appearance of an arutam to the vision-seeker.[20]

Some South American tobacco species normally contain large amounts or are brewed in such fashion as to have hallucinogenic amounts of nicotine.[21] But one of the members may drink an infusion of *maikua,* datura, instead of tobacco-water; datura is the hallucinogen specifically connected with puberty in North America and is used in Colombia and northward to the Aztec, southern California, and the American Southwest. "The other members of the group abstain from *maikua* in order to be able to restrain and protect the delirious person under its influence."[22]

They may keep up this fasting for as long as five days. If unsuccessful, they return home to make an attempt at a later date. If the arutam seeker is fortunate, however, he will awaken about midnight to find the stars gone from the sky, the earth trembling, and a great wind felling the trees of the forest amid thunder and lightning. To keep from being blown down, he grasps a tree trunk and waits the arutam. Shortly the arutam appears from the depths of the forest, often in the form a pair of large creatures [in circumstances suggesting a violent "primal scene"]. The particular animal forms can vary considerably, but some of the most common arutam include a pair of giant jaguars fighting one another as they roll over and over towards the vision seeker, or two anacondas doing the same.[23]

Sometimes the vision may be of a single gigantic severed human head, or a ball of fire drifting through the jungle toward the visionary. When it is twenty or thirty feet away, he must run quickly forward to touch the vision with his hand (or a little stick, as in "counting coup" in North America), whereupon it explodes and instantly disappears. But the vision-seeker may be frightened and run away instead, for the *arutam* is a fearsome dead ancestor who has killed many men.

Upon acquiring this arutam soul, the person feels a sudden power surge into his body, accompanied by a new self-confidence. This power, called *kakarma*, is believed to increase one's intelligence as well as simple physical strength, and also to make it difficult for the soul possessor to lie or commit other dishonorable acts.... When one has thus obtained an arutam soul, he generally is seized with a tremendous desire to kill. If the person is past puberty, it is ordinarily only a matter of a few months before he joins or organizes a killing expedition.[24]

A new *arutam* "locks in" the *kakarma*-power of a previous one. A man can have only two at a time,

but this "lock-in" feature of the new soul makes it possible for a person to accumulate the *power* of an indefinite number of previous souls. In other words, while the acquisition of the souls is consecutive, the acquisition of the power is cumulative. By repeatedly killing, one can continually accu-

mulate power through the replacement of old arutam souls with new ones.
This "trade-in" mechanism is an important feature because, when a person
has had the same arutam soul for four or five years, it tends to leave its
sleeping possessor to wander nightly through the forest. Sooner or later,
while it is thus drifting through the trees, another Jívaro will "steal it."[25]

For this reason it is well to get a new soul before the old one begins
its nocturnal wanderings; hence the felt need to participate in a
killing raid every few years.

Since a man with an arutam soul cannot die as the result of physical violence,
poisoning, or witchcraft, i.e., any interpersonal attack, a person who wishes
to kill a specific enemy attempts to steal his arutam soul away from him as
a prelude to assassinating him. This soul-stealing or capturing process in-
volves drinking large quantities of an infusion of natemA... beating a log
signal drum, and repeating the name of the intended victim. Then if the
enemy's arutam soul is wandering nocturnally, it may one night hear the
would-be assassin's call and, "taking pity" on his need for such a soul, enter
his body, never to return to the body of its former possessor.[26]

The natemA from which the infusion is made is Banisteriopsis Caapi,
or "vine of the spirits," a powerful hallucinogen, much in use in
Amazonia. But such a witchcraft murder is not the end of it, for then
there emerges a muisak or "avenging" soul, which "comes into
existence only when a person who has seen an arutam is killed,
whether by natural or supernatural means.... The sole reason for
being of a person's muisak is to avenge his death."[27] This is a further
reason for the apprehensiveness characteristic of the headhunter. A
muisak may sometimes appear to the sleeping murderer in the form
of a jaguar, at which he tries to seize the gun or lance he keeps by
his bed, to kill it; if he does not, the demon will eventually kill him.

The widely publicized practice of the Jívaro in shrinking human heads can
be well understood only with a knowledge of the muisak concept. A major
part of the belief and ritual associated with the shrunken head or tsantsa is
a direct effort to thwart the muisak in its mission of vengeance. The Jívaro
believe that the completion of the process of head-shrinking forces the

muisak, hovering alongside the retreating war expedition, to enter the head trophy.[28]

After the dramatic complexities of visionary and head-hunting souls, the ordinary personal soul of the Jívaro is something of an anticlimax.

The "true" or "ordinary" soul, the nëkás wakanI, is born at the same moment as the person and is possessed by every living Jívaro, male or female. The true soul is present in the living individual primarily in the form of one's blood. Bleeding is therefore viewed as a process of soul-loss. This soul is passive during a person's real life and apparently is of relatively little interest to the Jívaro in terms of their total native belief systems.[29]

Drug-induced visions and soul-stealing, and the taking of enemy heads, are far more interesting preoccupations for the Jívaro.

The arutam soul belief system contains a number of significant supernatural traits organized together into one internally logical complex. In this system the central idea of immunity from death is combined with such anthropologically well-known concepts as: a vision quest; a guardian spirit; eternal and multiple souls; a variety of generalized ancestor worship; reincarnation; soul-loss; soul-capture; nonshamanistic spirit possession; and a concept of personally-acquired impersonal power, kakarma, which resembles, but is not precisely identical to, the Oceanian mana. The concept of the muisak furnishes the rationale for head-taking and shrinking. . . . The Jívaro are so preoccupied with killing. . . that their two most emphasized types of souls, the muisak and the arutam soul, are supernatural devices, respectively for murdering and avoiding being murdered.[30]

The price of soul-stealing is perpetual anxiety, lest one's own soul be stolen.

 The Mundurucú are a Tupian-speaking people of Brazil, originally of the upper Tapajós in Paraguay. Although the colonists subdued them in 1795, they exploited the warlike Mundurucú as mercenaries against tribes of the Madeira and Tocantin River (e.g., the wild no-madic cannibal Paratintin, who make flutes of the tibiae of their victims). In turn, thus encouraged, for over a hundred years longer, the Mundurucú could continue their fierce warfare and headhunting, give blood transfusions: by giving blood so that someone can have more, the donor will have less. . . . A woman's long hair is much admired, but the price is high: a woman with long hair is thought always to be thin and wan, and she cannot expect to have vigor and strength. Sources of vitality are insufficient to grow long hair and still leave an individual with energy and a well-fleshed body.[39]

Thus, once again, hair is related to life force.

We have noted earlier the reciprocal relationship of headhunting and of scalping among Indians. James Mooney writes that

Throughout both Americas the ordinary trophy was the head, excepting in the frozen extremes of the Arctic regions and Patagonia. . . a fact that Friederici ascribes to the inhospitable nature of the environment. . . . The rapid spread of the scalping practice over the continent until it had completely superseded the earlier head-hunting, he ascribes to the changed conditions brought about by the introduction of European weapons and to the encouragement given by the colonial governments in offering premiums for scalps. As paid and equipped allies of French or English the Indian warriors organized their raids on a larger scale and extended their excursions to more remote points. The head being too unwieldy to carry any great distance, in addition to the burden of gun and ammunition, the more convenient scalp was evidence of victory and check for payment. In the Pequot War of 1636–37 the Puritans paid for Indian heads. Forty years later and thereafter they paid for scalps on a steadily rising market until in 1732 good Chaplain Frye eked out his ministerial salary by killing Indians at one hundred pounds per scalp. . . . With such encouragement the rapid spread of the custom is easily understood. As to the whites, it may be briefly stated that the borderman was a scalp-hunter as long as a border line existed.[40]

However, small tribes like the Wailaki of the extreme far west were still taking the whole head in contact times.[41] But Spier and Sapir write of the Wishram that "the characteristic mode of mutilating the enemy dead was to rip open the belly, cut off the head and set it down ten paces distant, and take the scalp. This is repeatedly cited in Simpson's account. [In the light of the ritual respect for slain animals and their bones, this positioning of the head should probably be seen as a sign of extreme disrespect.] To this we can now add

for which they became famous over half a continent. They were called *Pay-quiché*, "decapitators," by other tribes for their habit of preserving embalmed heads.[31] Except for the whites and the neighboring Apiacá, all other non-Mundurucú were considered by them as *pariwat*, game to be preyed upon in incessant raids. An enemy was not merely to be guarded against but was the proper object of attack, and they pursued this goal with extraordinary vigor, on foot journeys of over a thousand miles to the Mato Grosso, to the upper Madeira, and even to the distant mouth of the Amazon; they made bark canoes only to cross large rivers, and were gone sometimes for over six months. Present-day Mundurucú spoke to the anthropologist Murphy

at length and with great animation of their former prowess as warriors and of expeditions against other tribes in which the enemy men and women were killed and decapitated and their children stolen. Nothing about their own culture interested the Mundurucú as much as the extinct but still remembered patterns of warfare, and the older men were zealous informants. . . . As among the Indians of the North American Plains, youths sought openly for the excitement of war and looked upon it as a means of self-validation and aggrandizement of prestige.[32]

Mundurucú completely lacked any defensive psychology and looked upon themselves simply as aggressors and victors, and they were widely feared, for the

central object of the raid was the taking of enemy heads, and a strict protocol was observed in the preparation of the trophies. After killing an enemy man or woman, the warrior quickly decapitated the corpse. The spine was severed at the foramen magnum, but the skin was cut around the chest, shoulders, and back to leave a substantial flap below the point of severance. The excess skin compensated for the inevitable shrinkage that accompanied desiccation.[33]

The most important status among them was that of a taker of a trophy head, and he was given the title of *Dajeboiši*, "mother of the peccary," in allusion to their view of other tribes as being game animals. They believed in "the trophy head's power to attract game and to cause their numerical increase, and the head-hunter was so titled because of his obvious fertility promoting function.... The trophy head was believed to exert a powerful charm over the spirit protectors of the animal world and thus improved the supply and availability of game."[34] The theme is ancient and worldwide: the human head and the fertility of game animals.

Reichel-Dolmatoff has uncovered a rich cosmology and symbolism among the Tukana Indians, implicating the Sun, sexuality, and the animals. The yellow rays of *go'á-mëe*, the Sun Father, are his semen and fertilizing power, penetrating all realms of space. The name refers to bone, the skeleton that sustains the body and "constitutes the basis of the moral code," as well as the continuity of traditions and the conviction of their validity. "The bone-god is a penis," said an informant. Lightning is "the ejaculation of the Sun that can fertilize the land," and the *payá* (shaman) himself is believed to be able to produce lightning. They have an ideology of a kind of cosmic continence. "The quantity of [human – animal – social – cosmic] energy being fixed, man must remove what he needs only under certain circumstances and must convert this particle of 'borrowed' energy into a form that can be reincorporated into the circuit."[35] The *vai-mahse*, Master of Animals, is a phallic being in charge of the game animals, an important part of the circuit of energy; the Milky Way is envisaged as a vast area of semen and is the sphere of hallucinations, where the cosmic levels join. However, this view of an orderly universe does not give him any great peace of mind.

The Desana is not an individual we would call contented, balanced, and adjusted. His sense of being a man is dominated by the constant conflict between... his sexual impulses and the prohibitions that his culture imposes on him. The message of the Sun Father... is not simply a code designed to regulate sexual relationships... ; it has a much wider and deeper meaning for the culture.... In the cultural world of the Desana, men and animals live in a true symbiosis, a state of total interdependence, conceived in terms of one single cycle of fertility and procreation.... In various ritual activities man fertilizes nature, but at the price of a great sacrifice in the sphere of his

own sexuality. The fundamental rule of the hunter is sexual absti... this rule demands a level of repression that cannot but lead to profound anxiety.... Sexual repression has the double aim of fostering sexuality and the multiplication of the animals.... The s... is considered a great danger, a situation fraught with anguished... especially for the man who fears to lose his skill as a hunter.... The... of the Sun Father... is, above all, an exhortation to conserve energy.

The finiteness of the supply of energy, even in the whole co... constrains the Desana.

It is possible that these notions of conservation are widesp... even universal, among American Indians — although not all... nographies have the sensitivity to native cognitive structures or... completeness of Reichel-Dolmatoff's fieldwork. Nor do all grou... necessarily have the elaborate explicitness of the Desana. Howev... in North America, Adamson Hoebel reports of the Cheyenne a cle... concept of the finiteness of sexual energy and the need for care i... its conservation and expenditure.[37] In South America the male sub... stance is related to blood.

In Bororo belief, each person's health is dependent on a store of a type of life force, which is often equated with blood, general vitality, fertility, mental agility, and so forth. An individual's *rakare* is slowly accumulated during childhood and adolescence, but after sexual maturity it may be diminished in a number of ways, preeminently through the loss of body fluids such as semen. Frequent intercourse or masturbation is most debilitating for young men, who, since they are "soft" or incompletely formed, need to conserve their *rakare* to complete their growth and to withstand the rigors of aging.... The Bororo view seems to be both that intercourse in these [ritual] circumstances offends the spirits, who bring illness to the wrongdoer, and that it exhausts the personal forces which insure a measure of safety when dealing with the supernaturals.[38]

In Middle America the "image of limited good" applies specifically to blood.

Although best described for Guatemala, the belief that blood is non-regenerative is widespead in Latin America. This belief, frequently unverbalized, may be one of the reasons it is so difficult to persuade Latin Americans to for which they became famous over half a continent. They were called *Pay-quiché*, "decapitators," by other tribes for their habit of preserving embalmed heads.[31] Except for the whites and the neighboring Apiacá, all other non-Mundurucú were considered by them as *pariwat*, game to be preyed upon in incessant raids. An enemy was not merely to be guarded against but was the proper object of attack, and they pursued this goal with extraordinary vigor, on foot journeys of over a thousand miles to the Mato Grosso, to the upper Madeira, and even to the distant mouth of the Amazon; they made bark canoes only to cross large rivers, and were gone sometimes for over six months. Present-day Mundurucú spoke to the anthropologist Murphy

at length and with great animation of their former prowess as warriors and of expeditions against other tribes in which the enemy men and women were killed and decapitated and their children stolen. Nothing about their own culture interested the Mundurucú as much as the extinct but still remembered patterns of warfare, and the older men were zealous informants. . . . As among the Indians of the North American Plains, youths sought openly for the excitement of war and looked upon it as a means of self-validation and aggrandizement of prestige.[32]

Mundurucú completely lacked any defensive psychology and looked upon themselves simply as aggressors and victors, and they were widely feared, for the

central object of the raid was the taking of enemy heads, and a strict protocol was observed in the preparation of the trophies. After killing an enemy man or woman, the warrior quickly decapitated the corpse. The spine was severed at the foramen magnum, but the skin was cut around the chest, shoulders, and back to leave a substantial flap below the point of severance. The excess skin compensated for the inevitable shrinkage that accompanied desiccation.[33]

The most important status among them was that of a taker of a trophy head, and he was given the title of *Dajeboiši*, "mother of the peccary," in allusion to their view of other tribes as being game animals. They

believed in "the trophy head's power to attract game and to cause
their numerical increase, and the head-hunter was so titled because
of his obvious fertility promoting function.... The trophy head was
believed to exert a powerful charm over the spirit protectors of the
animal world and thus improved the supply and availability of
game."[34] The theme is ancient and worldwide: the human head and
the fertility of game animals.

Reichel-Dolmatoff has uncovered a rich cosmology and symbolism among the Tukana Indians, implicating the Sun, sexuality, and
the animals. The yellow rays of *go'á-mëe*, the Sun Father, are his
semen and fertilizing power, penetrating all realms of space. The
name refers to bone, the skeleton that sustains the body and "constitutes the basis of the moral code," as well as the continuity of
traditions and the conviction of their validity. "The bone-god is a
penis," said an informant. Lightning is "the ejaculation of the Sun
that can fertilize the land," and the *payá* (shaman) himself is believed
to be able to produce lightning. They have an ideology of a kind of
cosmic continence. "The quantity of [human – animal – social –
cosmic] energy being fixed, man must remove what he needs only
under certain circumstances and must convert this particle of 'borrowed' energy into a form that can be reincorporated into the circuit."[35] The *vai-mahse*, Master of Animals, is a phallic being in charge
of the game animals, an important part of the circuit of energy; the
Milky Way is envisaged as a vast area of semen and is the sphere of
hallucinations, where the cosmic levels join. However, this view of
an orderly universe does not give him any great peace of mind.

The Desana is not an individual we would call contented, balanced, and
adjusted. His sense of being a man is dominated by the constant conflict
between... his sexual impulses and the prohibitions that his culture imposes
on him. The message of the Sun Father... is not simply a code designed to
regulate sexual relationships... ; it has a much wider and deeper meaning
for the culture.... In the cultural world of the Desana, men and animals live
in a true symbiosis, a state of total interdependence, conceived in terms of
one single cycle of fertility and procreation.... In various ritual activities
man fertilizes nature, but at the price of a great sacrifice in the sphere of his

own sexuality. The fundamental rule of the hunter is sexual abstinence, and this rule demands a level of repression that cannot but lead to a state of profound anxiety.... Sexual repression has the double aim of magically fostering sexuality and the multiplication of the animals.... The sexual act is considered a great danger, a situation fraught with anguished images, especially for the man who fears to lose his skill as a hunter.... The message of the Sun Father... is, above all, an exhortation to conserve energy.[36]

The finiteness of the supply of energy, even in the whole cosmos, constrains the Desana.

It is possible that these notions of conservation are widespead, even universal, among American Indians — although not all ethnographies have the sensitivity to native cognitive structures or the completeness of Reichel-Dolmatoff's fieldwork. Nor do all groups necessarily have the elaborate explicitness of the Desana. However, in North America, Adamson Hoebel reports of the Cheyenne a clear concept of the finiteness of sexual energy and the need for care in its conservation and expenditure.[37] In South America the male substance is related to blood.

In Bororo belief, each person's health is dependent on a store of a type of life force, which is often equated with blood, general vitality, fertility, mental agility, and so forth. An individual's *rakare* is slowly accumulated during childhood and adolescence, but after sexual maturity it may be diminished in a number of ways, preeminently through the loss of body fluids such as semen. Frequent intercourse or masturbation is most debilitating for young men, who, since they are "soft" or incompletely formed, need to conserve their *rakare* to complete their growth and to withstand the rigors of aging.... The Bororo view seems to be both that intercourse in these [ritual] circumstances offends the spirits, who bring illness to the wrongdoer, and that it exhausts the personal forces which insure a measure of safety when dealing with the supernaturals.[38]

In Middle America the "image of limited good" applies specifically to blood.

Although best described for Guatemala, the belief that blood is non-regenerative is widespread in Latin America. This belief, frequently unverbalized, may be one of the reasons it is so difficult to persuade Latin Americans to give blood transfusions: by giving blood so that someone can have more, the donor will have less. . . . A woman's long hair is much admired, but the price is high: a woman with long hair is thought always to be thin and wan, and she cannot expect to have vigor and strength. Sources of vitality are insufficient to grow long hair and still leave an individual with energy and a well-fleshed body.[39]

Thus, once again, hair is related to life force.

We have noted earlier the reciprocal relationship of headhunting and of scalping among Indians. James Mooney writes that

Throughout both Americas the ordinary trophy was the head, excepting in the frozen extremes of the Arctic regions and Patagonia . . . a fact that Friederici ascribes to the inhospitable nature of the environment. . . . The rapid spread of the scalping practice over the continent until it had completely superseded the earlier head-hunting, he ascribes to the changed conditions brought about by the introduction of European weapons and to the encouragement given by the colonial governments in offering premiums for scalps. As paid and equipped allies of French or English the Indian warriors organized their raids on a larger scale and extended their excursions to more remote points. The head being too unwieldy to carry any great distance, in addition to the burden of gun and ammunition, the more convenient scalp was evidence of victory and check for payment. In the Pequot War of 1636 – 37 the Puritans paid for Indian heads. Forty years later and thereafter they paid for scalps on a steadily rising market until in 1732 good Chaplain Frye eked out his ministerial salary by killing Indians at one hundred pounds per scalp. . . . With such encouragement the rapid spread of the custom is easily understood. As to the whites, it may be briefly stated that the borderman was a scalp-hunter as long as a border line existed.[40]

However, small tribes like the Wailaki of the extreme far west were still taking the whole head in contact times.[41] But Spier and Sapir write of the Wishram that "the characteristic mode of mutilating the enemy dead was to rip open the belly, cut off the head and set it down ten paces distant, and take the scalp. This is repeatedly cited in Simpson's account. [In the light of the ritual respect for slain animals and their bones, this positioning of the head should probably be seen as a sign of extreme disrespect.] To this we can now add that by way of trophies the Wishram took the scalp, hands, feet, and sometimes penis and testes, but not the head. The scalp was of generous size, the whole head skin above ears and eyes, not the mere vortex on the crown taken by Plains tribes."[42] The ubiquitous "scalp dance" of North American Indians should not be thought of as simply a celebration of war victory or a display of personal prowess. The scalp dance had the practical purpose of decontaminating or domesticating the power resident in the enemy scalp — much as the new *arutam* of a Jívaro headhunter was to bind in the *kakarma* power of an earlier one and to "fix" in the shrunken head-skin the *muisak* revenge-soul of a slain victim. Even the "peaceful Pueblos" therefore had to have the scalp ceremonial.[43]

Another way for Indians to get medicine power was to steal it, sexually or ritually. Previously, Plains Americanists have thought the seduction of the wife of a member of a warriors' society ranking higher than one's own was merely a matter of bravado, somewhat like "counting coup" on a live enemy, in exposing oneself to the danger of reprisal. However, the careful work of Alice Kehoe reveals other possible dimensions of meaning. "Sexual intimacy as a means of transferring spiritual power appears to have been a Mandan-Hidatsa ceremonial trait borrowed by three Algonkian Plains tribes as part of the graded men's societies complex."[44] Lowie noted that the men's societies of five northern tribes (Mandan, Hidatsa, Arapaho, Atsina or Gros Ventres, and Blackfoot) differed from those of other Plains tribes in having strict grading, general age-status, and the purchase of membership. "As part of the purchase price the buyer ceremonially surrenders his wife to the older man in some, at least, of the societies in each tribe."[45] Mandan belief in power transfer through sexual intercourse was notorious during the fur-trading period, according to Bowers and Bruner, and the physical anthropologist Newman explained the blondness of many Mandan as probably the consequence of an appreciable gene-pool modification in pursuit of the desired power-transfer.[46] Lowie and Bowers, as much earlier

Lewis and Clark and Maximilian had, described "the Mandan and Hidatsa custom of a man desiring power offering his wife to an older man of recognized power, who was felt to confer a favor upon the younger man by transmitting some power through the woman."[47] The custom is evidently of immense antiquity, for it is implicated with a symbolic animal coitus of the woman with the power-giving buffalo—which immediately recalls many Old Stone Age engravings (e.g., the famous "reindeer-wives") of animal–human intercourse.[48]

For the Mandan, symbolic intercourse with the bison ("Walking With the Buffaloes") represented the origin and essence of human society. Okipa ceremony myths claimed that the ceremony's Buffalo Dance was one of the most ancient Mandan rituals, practiced at a period when the people had not yet developed tools, complex social organization, or the many later ceremonials. The Buffalo Dance, and accompanying Okipa rites, was believed to bring abundant bison herds and prosperity to the villages. Intercourse between a respectable matron and a man of power drew to the woman, and her marital partner, some of the power flowing from the primal bison; this concept was clearly demonstrated in the bison-calling ceremonies, in which women made the motion of physically pulling the power from a bundle-owner into their bodies.[49]

The Hidatsa added another element of symbolism.

Relinquishing a wife to a father's clansman reinforced the special position of the father's clan as the proper source of religious knowledge and consequent spiritual power. A man received his physical being by the act of intercourse between his father and his mother, then his adult life was strengthened and enhanced by intercourse between his "fathers," in the extended sense of father's clansmen, and the woman who filled the role of mother in the lodge.[50]

Algonkian borrowers of ritual Mandan-Hidatsa sexual intercourse had more attenuated symbols and ceremonies. The Arapaho "Transferrer," symbolizing the Sun, was supposed to have coitus with the wife of the Sun Dance sponsor, and a root representing seed was passed from mouth to mouth; Dorsey's informant said the ceremonial "straight-pipe is the penis or root of the man."[51] The Cheyenne rite remained symbolic only, the ritual couple merely being together covered with a buffalo robe. The Gros Ventre "grandfather" emphatically did not have coitus with his "granddaughter" but merely prayed with a ceremonial tobacco pipe that the Above-Persons would bless the woman; passed the root from mouth to mouth; and painted the nude bodies of his "grandchildren" each morning before the day's ceremonies began.[52]

The Blackfoot, the most distant from the Missouri River village tribes, had the most attenuated but still plainly symbolic form of the rite, and used it only in the purchase of membership in the highest-ranking Horn Society of the Blood tribe.

At the culmination of the prayer, the "father" touches his penis to the woman's vulva. The rite is continued past this point only if the woman is known to be virtuous and her husband is a worthy man. If such is the opinion of the "father," he next bends his forefinger into the shape of a horn, bellows like a bison bull, and finally has coitus with the woman, transferring a piece of prairie turnip from his mouth to hers during the act. . . . Her "father" ends the rite, and the fast, by painting her, one pattern indicating performance of only the first half of the ritual, another pattern indicating completion of the entire ritual and, therefore, honor to the woman and her husband.[53]

The grave symbolism of the sacred rite is emphasized by the high value the Blackfoot place upon chastity.

Virtuous women would publicly proclaim their chastity by coming forward to claim the right to help cut up the perfect bison tongues used in the Sun Dance. A woman's announcement often included naming the men whose attempts at seduction she had repulsed. . . . The steadfast, disciplined character demonstrated by an unsullied woman was comparable to the firm courage of a warrior, and indeed, the women proclaimed their chastity in the manner of men recounting their coups.[54]

The significance of the ritual is emphasized also by "the awesome power of the Blood Horns," which surpassed that of even the most powerful Blackfoot shamans. "The form of the bison fertility ritual is retained by the Blackfoot, but it has ceased to signify the physical transfer of power. . .; it has become a frightening demonstration of the power that can be wielded by the comrades of the Horn."[55] For the horn, sprouting from the life-containing head of animals, is from the Old Stone Age onward the most sacred symbol of male power and fertility.[56] (The ancient Shinto ritual of the reindeer horns at Nara and the Chinese use of powdered horn as male potency-restorer are not unrelated.)[57]

In both Americas, another much-developed way to get supernatural power from outside was to imbibe a wide variety of psychotropic and hallucinogenic drugs, often in connection with religious cults. Indians knew aboriginally nearly a hundred psychotropic drugs, as opposed to a mere handful in the Old World. Some, like the Red Bean *(Sophora secundiflora)* were very old: the Bonfire Shelter beans in Texas had a C_{14} date of 8440 – 8120 B.C. and were found in direct association with Folsom points and the bones of an extinct bison; Frightful Cave in northern Mexico yielded red beans dating from 7500 B.C., at least as ancient as the paleo-Indian "big game" hunters of the earliest Americans.[58] Myths of lightning-engendered mushrooms (and by an eagle-thunderbird) in both Eurasia and America, and the shamanic use of the same *Amanita muscaria* as the earliest Aryan *soma* also by central Algonkians, even suggest Mesolithic horizons that, on other grounds, can be confidently asserted of the earliest Indian migrants from Siberia.[59]

Indian psychotropic drugs were often connected with puberty ceremonials, for example, jimson weed (datura) in California and the Southwest southward to the Andean region; and the "Black Drink" *(Ilex* spp., botanically related to *maté,* "Paraguayan tea") used in pubertal "huskinawing," on the Atlantic seaboard from Chesapeake Bay into the Gulf of Mexico coast of Texas. The earliest known to Europeans was the narcotic snuff *yopo (Anadenanthera peregrina),* used in the Antilles and Orinoco basin; but there are also the narcotic snuffs *yakee* and *parica (Virola* spp.) of the Orinoco, *huilca* of Peruvian Amazonia, and *rapé (Olmedeoperbea sclerophylla)* of Brazilian Amazonia. The oldest narcotic known to American archeology is *Ungnadia speciosa* of prehistoric trans-Pecos Texas and northern Mexico.[60] Next to tobacco (*Nicotiana* spp.), universally used ritually by Indians from mid-latitude Canada to Patagonia — i.e., anywhere the plants will grow — the most widespread native psychotropic plant used nowadays is *peyote* (*Lophophora williamsii*, which contains thirty-some psychotropic alkaloids), earlier of prehistoric Mexico and the southern Plains, but now in religious cult use northward into Canada and westward into California. The "lost" Aztec narcotic mushroom *teonanácatl* comprises a half-dozen psilocybin-containing *Stropharia* species, still in modern use by the Mazatec and a half-dozen other Mexican tribes. The Mazatec of Oaxaca also have a psychotropic mint, *Salvia divinorum*. But I have listed here only a small fraction of these native Indian drugs.

Perhaps the greatest known concentration of aboriginal narcotics (but native Colombian and Lake Titicaca tribes might run them a close second, were they as fully studied) was found among the Aztec, who had *toloache* datura, a psilocybin *teonanácatl*, *peyotl* (*Lophophora* spp.), *ololiuqui* (*Rivea corymbosa*, a morning glory whose seeds contain an LSD-like substance), and a dozen others, some still unidentified botanically.[61]

As to large areal diffusion—again, after tobacco—*coca* (*Erythroxylon Coca*, source of cocaine) was pan-Andean aboriginally. *Ayahuasca, caapi, yajé* (*Banisteriopsis* spp.) was used in both tropical Amazonia and the Orinoco drainage. Ceremonial drunkenness on native undistilled beers and wines extended from the non-Pueblo Southwest through Central America to the mid-Andes (and in Amazonia in Jívaro headhunters' victory feasts and elsewhere in Brazilian funereal spirit-feasts).[62]

A mescaline-containing Peruvian "San Pedro" cactus (*Trichocereus pachanoi*) has been found by recent ethnographers to have been widely used by Peruvian and Ecuadorean shamans since prehistoric times; and Gordon Wasson recently discovered an Ojibwa shamaness using *Amanita muscaria* mushrooms. American Indians have even discovered the narcotic properties of introduced non-native plants such as *Genista canariensis,* used decoratively by florists — which has suggested to one student that, in their high evaluation of the vision-quest in conducting their lives, American Indians are in a sense "culturally programmed" for the discovery and use of mind-altering drugs.[63] Indeed, to the American Indian, *any* plant that can move life-consciousness in the human head must by that token contain supernatural power to be held in holy awe.

Notes

1. Ruth Benedict, "The Vision in Plains Culture," *American Anthropologist* (1922), 24:1 – 23; W. La Barre, *The Ghost Dance: Origins of Religion* (New York: Doubleday, 1970), p. 43; see also pp. 128, 131 – 32.

2. La Barre, *Ghost Dance,* p. 136 — though the Tukuna, for example, had a vision-quest much like the North American; see C. Nimuendajú, *The Tucuna,* University of California Publications in American Archeology and Ethnology, (1952) no. 45; see also Nimuendajú, "The Tucuna," in J. Steward, ed., *Handbook of South American Indians,* 3:713 – 25, Bureau of American Ethnology, Bulletin 143, 8 vols. (Washington, 1946 – 1959), 3:724 – 25. The difference is evidently only in the greater *political* power of shamans in South America. Werner Stenzel, "Tetzavitl, Evidences for the Vision Quest among the Aztecs," *Wiener Völkerkundliche Mitteilungen,* 14-15 JG., N. F. vol. 9/10, 1967-1968; cf. Stenzel, "The Sacred Bundles in Mesoamerican Religion," *Verhandlungen des 38 Internationalen Amerikanistenkongress,* vol. 2, Stuttgart, 1970; Stenzel, "The Consecration of Ancient Mexican Rulers," ms. 1970, a ceremony that retains ritual elements of the old vision-quest and medicine-bundles as well. See also A. Hvidtfeldt, *Teotl and *Ixipatli: Some Central Conceptions in Ancient Mexican Religion* (Copenhagen: Munksgaard, 1958), pp. 52, 76, 97, 118, 140.

3. La Barre, *Ghost Dance,* pp. 43, 132 – 33, 136, 140 – 41. The guardian spirit sought in the vision-quest is found in "eastern Siberia, across the length and breadth of North America, and down into South America." Ruth Benedict, *The Concept of the Guardian Spirit in North America,* Memoirs of the American Anthropological Association no. 29 (1923), p. 9.

4. La Barre, *Ghost Dance*, p. 363; for the *berdache*, see pp. 138–40, 156 –57, 179–81.

5. La Barre, *Ghost Dance*, pp. 130–31; also pp. 133–34. But see La Barre, *Culture in Context* (Durham, N.C.: Duke University Press, 1980), p. 74. Aztec warfare to get spirit-food for the gods is the *native* (emic) reason—and that humans can make war from irrational motives is a proposition to be accepted with equanimity by Freudians. But scientizing Marxists insist that ultimate "real" motivation must be etic–rational (and invariably economic). Michael Harner ("The Ecological Basis for Aztec Sacrifice," *American Ethnologist* [1977] 4:117 – 35) and Marvin Harris (*Cannibals and Kings*, [New York: Vintage, 1977]) propose a cultural – materialist rationale for Aztec human sacrifice as providing raw material for elitist cannibalism (a tendentious symbolism to be sure). B. R. Ortiz de Montellano thinks Harner greatly overestimates the number on Aztec skull-racks, and argues that even this large number of victims would not have given a significant amount of protein to the Aztec elite, much less commoners too. "Counting Skulls: Comment on the Aztec Cannibalism Theory of Harner–Harris," *American Anthropologist* (1983), 84(2):403–6. Besides, the time of consumption was not periods of scarcity but times of thanksgiving and plenty. Ortiz, "Aztec Cannibalism: An Ecological Necessity?" *Science* (1978), 200:611 – 17). Ethnologist Jacques Soustelle (*Daily Life of the Aztec on the Eve of the Spanish Conquest* [Harmondsworth, England: Penguin Books, 1964]) and C. Duverger (*La Fleur Létale: Economie de Sacrifice Azteque* [Paris: Seuil, 1978], pp. 184–87, 200 – 203) agree that Aztec sacrifice and cannibalism took place but consider their extent and significance controversial. George P. Castile, while admiring Harner's "nomothetic" approach, scouts any notion that Harner has proven his case. "Purple People Eaters?: A Comment on Elite Class Cannibalism à la Harner–Harris," *American Anthropologist* (1980) 82:389–91.

Barry Isaac argues that tribute, not captives, was the prime concern of the elite who guided policy, yet "it would be misleading to ignore the ritual component of Aztec warfare" when the ordinary soldier saw warfare as a way to get captives for later ritual sacrifice. "Aztec Warfare: Goals and Battlefield Comportment," *Ethnology* [1983], 22(2):121 – 31. To what lengths will "objectivists" go to distort motives they find uncomfortably irrational: they will themselves be irrational to prove that irrationality cannot be. Certainly contact-period ethnography makes central this irrational religious motive for war; elitist cannibal calories may be wholly a rationalizing Marxist invention. The physical anthropologist Stanley Garn seriously questioned cannibalism as a cost-effective procedure anyway. "The Noneconomic Nature of Eating People," *American Anthropologist* [1979], 81:902 – 3. Nathan Elberg, curiously, taxes Garn and not Harner ("Aztec Cannibalism and the Calorific Obsession," *American Anthropologist,* [1981], 83:622), and thinks Garn's arguments do not negate Harner's; evidently Marxist arguments are not vulnerable to logical controversion. And yet, if Marxists insist upon an economic – rationalist motive as the real reason for Aztec warfare, they must surely attend to Garn's reasoning that cannibalism is, in fact, *not* economic.

The controversy has extended even to questioning the logic of the 1976 Nobel Prize winner in Physiology/Medicine, Carleton Gajdusek. Lyle Steadman and Charles Merbs state that "the use of cannibalism to account for the transmission of *kuru* [a progressive and invariably fatal neurophysiological disease of the Fore tribe of montane New Guinea believed to be due to a slow-acting virus] has now received virtually universal acceptance." "Kuru and Cannibalism?" *American Anthropologist* (1982), 84:611 – 27, p. 615 — a review of *Kuru: Early Letters and Field-Notes from the Collection of D. Carleton Gajdusek* (New York: Raven Press, 1981). Gajdusek himself early had doubts whether the Fore endocannibalistic eating of dead relatives was the responsible vector, and in his Nobel Prize address in Stockholm in 1976 said only that "we believe that contamination during the cannibalistic ritual was the sole source of transmission of kuru from man to man" (quoted by Steadman and Merbs, p. 615). Since Fore women handle the heads and the corpses, women and their children are the chief sufferers from *kuru;* no cases in patients under twenty have occurred since 1967, after authorities enjoined burial of the dead. Since the virus may conceivably be transmitted either percutaneously or through mucosa (e.g. the eyes), "the act of cannibalism may be irrelevant to the transmission of kuru" (p. 619). Unfortunately, we do not know the Fore rationale for their alleged eating of brains, whatever the hints elsewhere in montane New Guinea that *muelos* concepts may be involved.

Recently, Arens has argued that supposed cannibalism is merely a tendentious attribution of repulsive behavior to the unknown or the enemy tribe and only dubiously existed in ethnographic fact, W. Arens, *The Man-Eating Myth: Anthropology and Anthropophagy* (New York: Oxford University Press, 1978). While the canard hypothesis may frequently be correct, the refutation of *Aztec cannibalism* demolishes a straw man, since Aztec collected victims' heads *to feed soul-stuff to their gods,* according to plentiful contact-period information. That *communicants ate* the victims' bodies — presumably because of regional protein deficiency — appears to be an invention of modern Marxists, explaining by formula what probably never existed ethnographically. We do not need to rationalize economically what was irrationally motivated religiously (that is, by adding onto well-proven headhunting a merely supposititious cannibalism of the whole body). Meanwhile, by casting doubt on the Aztec and a few other alleged practitioners of cannibalism, Arens does not make a logical case for the nonexistence of cannibalism anywhere. In this review of Arens, Ivan Brady writes: "Can we conclude rationally or persuasively from this exercise that cannibalism does not exist in other than an emergency or exceptional form? I think not, at least not without cavalierly dismissing the reality and importance of the belief system." ("The Myth-Eating Man," *American Anthropologist* (1982), 84:595 – 611), p. 606.

Indeed, any behavior, however repugnant, which one human being is physically capable of performing, stands a chance of being somewhere culturally institutionalized; and for so common a fantasy as cannibalism, probably the fact has occurred many times. I consider cannibalism probable at one time among West Africans, Middle and South American Indians, Melanesians of Papua New Guinea and the Melanesian islands, and some Polynesians (where "protein deficiency" may have in fact occurred, e.g., in a few high islands like the Marquesas that lacked coral reefs and fish). Cannibalism of parts of an enemy's body in order to incorporate his qualitites seems to me even more firmly authenticated. But the evidence in each case must be scrupulously examined, since Arens' argument has merit. The whole question of cannibalism is to be reviewed in a future issue of *Ethos*.

6. Christopher L. Moser, *Human Decapitation in Ancient Mesoamerica*, Studies in Precolumbian Art and Archeology, no. 11 (Washington: Dumbarton Oaks, 1973), pp. 4 – 72 p. 5; for Mesoamerican headhunting tribes, pp. 7, 12, 26, 28; and Ralph L. Beals, "The Comparative Ethnology of Northern Mexico before 1750," *Ibero-Americana*, 1932 no. 2; and Beals, "The Acaxee: A Mountain Tribe of Durango and Sinaloa," *Ibero-Americana*, 1933, no. 6.

7. Moser, "Human Decapitation," p. 49; wearing of heads, p. 23

8. Moser, "Human Decapitation," pp. 47, 48; pulque and maguey, p. 39; earth-fertility goddesses, p. 35.

9. Moser, "Human Decapitation," p. 50.

10. Åke Hultkrantz, *The Religions of the American Indians* (Berkeley: University of California Press, 1979), pp. 141 – 42. Hultkrantz compares the Miami care in not injuring ears of corn in harvesting with "the rule that the hunters harming the bones of the animal means loss of luck in the chase" (p. 143). European prehistorians and ethnologists have documented especially well this earliest of religious rites, the bone-cult "rite at the site" of a

kill or placation of animal prey: Ivar Paulsen, "Zur Aufbewahrung der Tierknochen im nördlichen Nordamerika," *Mitteilungen aus dem Museum für Völkerkunde in Hamburg* (1959), 25:182 – 88; B. Bonnerjea, "Hunting Superstitions of the American Aborigines," *Internationales Archiv für Ethnographie* (1934), 32:157 – 84. These American Indian customs are widely paralleled in Europe and Asia — Shor, Evenk, Goldi, Orochi, Itel'men, etc., of Siberia: M. G. Levin and L. P. Potapov, eds., *The Peoples of Siberia,* (Chicago: University of Chicago Press, 1964) pp. 464, 649, 711, 757, 879. See also I. Paulsen, "Die Tierknochen im Jagdritual der nordeurasiatischer Völker," *Zeitschrift für Ethnologie* (1959), 84:270-93; Adolf Friedrich, "Knochen und Skelette in der Vorstellungswelt Nordasiens, *Wiener Beiträge zur Kulturgeschichte und Linguistik* (1943), 5; Friedrich, "Die Forschung über das fruhzeitlich Jägertum," *Paideuma* (1941), 2:20 – 43; Uno Holmburg-Harva, "Uber der Jagdriten der nordlischen Völkers Asiens und Europas," *Journal de la Société Finno-Ougrienne* [Helsinki] (1925), 61:1 – 53; Carl-Martin Edsman, [Referat:] "Studien zur Religion des Jägers," to "Studier i jägarens religion," *Annales Academiae Regiae Scientiarum Upsaliensis, Kunglik Vetenskapssamhällets i Uppsala, Årsbok* (1958), 2:33 – 94; and F. Gahs, "Köpf-, Schädel- und Langbeinknochenopfer bei den Rentiervölkern," in W. Koppers, ed., *Publication d'hommage offerte au P[ère] W. Schmidt* pp. 231 – 68 (Vienna: Mechitharisten-Congregations-Buchdruckerei, 1928). Bone marrow is the necessary seed for the reconstitution of slain prey.

11. Alice S. Straus, "Northern Cheyenne Ethnopsychology," *Ethos* (1977), 5:325 – 57, p. 327.

12. R. H. Lowie, *The Assiniboine,* American Museum of Natural History, Anthropological Papers no. 17 (New York, 1909), p. 225.

13. R. B. Onians, *The Origins of European Thought* (New York: Arno Press, 1973), pp. 125, 130, 229, 231 – 33, 235 n. 4.

14. Levin and Potapov, *Peoples of Siberia,* p. 64; review by D. S. Davidson, *American Anthropologist* (1938), 40:160. The Alvastra (Sweden) Neolithic skull shows evidence of scalping; see H. Hamperl and W. S. Laughlin, "Osteological Consequences of Scalping," *Human Biology* (1959), 31:80 – 89, cited in Folke Henschen, *The Human Skull: A Cultural History* (New York: Praeger, 1966), p. 10.

15. G. Friederici, *Skalpierung und ähnliche Kriegesgebräuche in Amerika* (Brunswick: Viewig, 1936); La Barre, *Ghost Dance,* pp. 133, 153 n. 16.

16. Ruth Underhill, *Indians of the Pacific North West* (Riverside: Calif.: Educational Division of the U.S. Office of Indian Affairs, 1945), p. 182.

17. Bertrand Flornoy, *Jívaro: Among the Head-Shrinkers of the Amazon,* Jean Pace, trans. (New York: Elek, 1953); Rafael Karsten, "The Head-Hunters of Western Amazonas: The Life and Culture of the Jíbaro Indians of Eastern Ecuador and Peru," *Societas Scientarum Fennica, Commentationes Humanarum Litterarum* (Helsinki) (1935), vol. 7, no. 1.; J. H. Steward and A. Métraux, "Tribes of the Peruvian and Ecuadorian Montaña," in J. H. Steward, ed., *Handbook of South American Indians,* Bureau of American Ethnology, Bulletin 143, vol. 3, 1948; M. W. Stirling, "Historical and Ethnographical Material on the Jívaro Indians," Bureau of American Ethnology, Bulletin 117 (1938); and F. W. Up de Graff, *Head Hunters of the Amazon* (New York: Duffield, 1923), pp. 272–83.

18. La Barre, *Ghost Dance,* pp. 155–56 n. 20

19. Michael J. Harner, "Jívaro Souls," *American Anthropologist* (1962), 64:258–72, p. 258.

20. Harner, "Jívaro Souls," p. 260.

21. Johannes Wilbert, "Tobacco and Shamanistic Ecstasy among the Warao Indians of Venezuela," in Peter T. Furst, ed., *Flesh of the Gods: The Ritual Use of Hallucinogens,* pp. 55–83 (New York: Praeger, 1972).

22. Harner, "Jívaro Souls," p. 271n.7.

23. Harner, "Jívaro Souls," pp. 260–61.

24. Harner, "Jívaro Souls," p. 261.

25. Harner, "Jívaro Souls," p. 262.

26. Harner, "Jívaro Souls," pp. 262–63.

27. Harner, "Jívaro Souls," p. 264. For recent fieldwork in South America on the use of *Banisteriopsis* spp., see M. J. Harner, ed., *Hallucinogens and Shamanism* (New York: Oxford University Press, 1963); and Gerardo Reichel-Dolmatoff, "The Cultural Context of an Aboriginal Hallucinogen: *Banisteriopsis Caapi,*" in Furst, *Flesh of the Gods,* pp. 84–113.

28. Harner, "Jívaro Souls," p. 265.

29. Harner, "Jívaro Souls," p. 266.

30. Harner, "Jívaro Souls," p. 268.

31. G. E. Church, *Aborigines of South America* (London: Chapman & Hall, 1912).

32. Robert J. Murphy, "Intergroup Hostility and Social Cohesion," *American Anthropologist* (1957), 59:1018–35, pp. 1021–22.

33. Murphy, "Intergroup Hostility," p. 1023.

34. Murphy, "Intergroup Hostility," p. 1024.

35. Gerardo Reichel-Dolmatoff, *Amazonian Cosmos: The Sexual and*

Religious Symbolism of the Tukana Indians (Chicago: University of Chicago Press, 1971), pp. 48 – 50.

36. Reichel-Dolmatoff, *Amazonian Cosmos*, pp. 67 – 68.

37. E. Adamson Hoebel, *The Cheyennes* (New York: H. Holt, 1960), p. 84.

38. Christopher Crocker, "Men's House Associates among the Eastern Bororo," *Southwest Journal of Anthropology* (1969), 24:236 – 60, p. 241.

39. George M. Foster, "Peasant Society and the Image of Limited Good," *American Anthropologist* (1965), 67:293 – 315, p. 300.

40. James Mooney, review of Friederici, *Skalpieren und ähnliche Kriegesgebräuche*, in *American Anthropologist* (1907), 9:185 – 87; also in Frederica De Laguna, ed., *Selected Papers from the American Anthropologist 1888 – 1920* (Evanston, Ill., and Elmsford, N.Y., 1960), pp. 665 – 67.

41. Frederick W. Hodge, ed., *Handbook of American Indians North of Mexico*, Bureau of American Ethnology, Bulletin 30, (Washington, 1907), *s.v.* "Wailaki," p. 894a.

42. Leslie Spier and Edward Sapir, *Wishram Ethnography*, Washington [State] University Publications in Anthropology, vol. 3, no. 3, (1930), p. 231.

43. Elsie Clews Parsons, *The Scalp Ceremonial of Zuñi*, American Anthropological Association, Memoir 31, (1924).

44. Alice Kehoe, "The Functions of Ceremonial Sexual Intercourse Among the Northern Plains Indians," *Plains Anthropologist* (1970), 15(48):99 – 103, p. 99.

45. R. H. Lowie, *Plains Indian Age Societies*, American Museum of Natural History Anthropological Papers no. 11, part 13, (New York, 1916), p. 919.

46. A. W. Bowers, *Mandan Social and Ceremonial Organization* (Chicago: University of Chicago Press, 1950), pp. 117 – 122, 336 – 37, 462 – 63; E. M. Brunner, "Mandan," in E. H. Spicer, ed., *Perspectives in American Indian Culture Change*, pp. 187 – 277 (Chicago: University of Chicago Press, 1961), p. 232; and M. T. Newman, "The Blond Mandan: A Critical Review of an Old Problem," *Southwestern Journal of Anthropology* (1950), 6:255 – 72, p. 259.

47. Kehoe, "Ceremonial Sexual Intercourse," p. 99, citing R. H. Lowie, *Societies of the Crow, Hidatsa and Mandan Indians* American Museum of Natural History Anthropological Papers no. 11, part 3 (New York, 1913); Lowie, *Notes on the Social Organization and Customs of the Mandan, Hidatsa, and Crow Indians, ibid.,* no. 21, part 1, 1917.

48. La Barre, *Ghost Dance*, p. 425 nn. 20, 21. See also Matthew Stirling, "Stone Monuments of the Rio Chiquito, Vera Cruz, Mexico," (New York:

American Museum of Natural History, 43 (1955) 1–23, p. 19, pl. 25) showing jaguar – woman coitus discussed in P. T. Furst, "The Olmec Were-Jaguar Motif in the Light of Ethnographic Reality" (Washington: Dumbarton Oaks Conference on the Olmec, 1968).

49. Kehoe, "Ceremonial Sexual Intercourse," p. 100, citing Bowers, *Mandan*, pp. 117–22, 335–36.

50. Kehoe, "Ceremonial Sexual Intercourse," p. 100, citing Lowie, *Social Organization*, p. 40, and Lowie, *Societies*, pp. 228–29.

51. G. A. Dorsey, *The Arapaho Sun Dance*, Field Columbian Museum Publication no. 75, Anthropological Series vol. 4, (Chicago, 1903), pp. 176–78.

52. R. Flannery, *The Gros Ventre of Montana*, Catholic University Anthropological Papers, no. 1, part 4, (New York, 1957), pp. 214–15.

53. Kehoe, "Ceremonial Sexual Intercourse," p. 102.

54. Kehoe, "Ceremonial Sexual Intercourse"; Clark Wissler, *The Sun Dance of the Blackfoot Indians*, American Museum of Natural History Anthropological Papers no. 16, part 3 (New York, 1918), p. 240.

55. Kehoe, "Ceremonial Sexual Intercourse," p. 102. The repeated references in Kehoe's sources to coitus with the buffalo (and to such obtaining of buffalo power) forcibly recalls the numerous Paleolithic cave drawings of animal – human coitus and the "Reindeer Wife" (La Barre, *Ghost Dance*, p. 425). In this linking of modern American Indian and Old Stone Age symbolism, only the animals (deer and buffalo) differ. Again, in the famous north African Late Paleolithic (post – Capsian – Aurignacian) hunting scene, a line drawn from the hunter's bow to the vulva of his far-distant wife at home unmistakably links hunting and coitus, a Paleolithic symbolism also present in American Indian mythology (e.g., the deer on which the hunter draws his bow suddenly turns into a beautiful woman).

56. La Barre, *Ghost Dance*, pp. 194 n. 40, 399, 413–14, 417.

57. La Barre, *Ghost Dance*, pp. 429–30 n. 68.

58. P. T. Furst, "Archeological Evidences for Snuffing in Prehistoric Mexico," [Harvard] *Botanical Museum Leaflets* (July 31, 1974), 24(1):1–28, pp. 23–24; Furst, "Morning Glory and Mother Goddess at Tepantitla," in *Mesoamerican Archaeology*, pp. 190–91.

59. Summaries of American Indian psychotropic drug use: Richard Evans Schultes, "An Overview of Hallucinogens in the Western Hemisphere," in Furst, *Flesh of the Gods*, pp. 3–54; W. La Barre "Hallucinogens and the Shamanic Origins of Religion," pp. 261–78; La Barre, "Anthropological Perspectives on Hallucination, Hallucinogens, and the Shamanic Origins of

Religion," in *Culture in Context*, pp. 37–92; La Barre, "History and Ethnography of Cannabis," in *Culture in Context*, pp. 93 – 167; La Barre, *Ghost Dance*, pp. 143 – 49, 158 – 60 nn. 36 – 41. On *Amanita muscaria*, see La Barre, "Soma: The Three-and-One-Half Millennia Mystery," in *Culture in Context*, pp. 108 – 15.

60. J. M. Adovasio and G. F. Frey, "Prehistoric Psychotropic Drug Use in Northeastern Mexico and Trans-Pecos Texas," *Economic Botany* (1976), 30:94 – 96.

61. Richard Evans Schultes, "Mexico and Colombia: Two Major Centers of Aboriginal Use of Hallucinogens," *Journal of Psychedelic Drugs*, (1977), 9:173 – 76; see also W. La Barre, *ibid.* (1977), 9:351.

62. W. La Barre, "Native American Beers," *American Anthropologist*, (1938), 40:224 – 34; Ruth Bunzel, "The Role of Alcoholism in two Central American Cultures," *Psychiatry*, (1940), 3:361 – 87; R. C. Dailey, "The Role of Alcohol among North American Indians as Reported in the Jesuit Relations," *Anthropologica* (1968), 10(1):45 – 59; and E. S. Carpenter, "Alcohol in the Iroquois Dream Quest," *American Journal of Psychiatry* (1959), 116:148 – 51.

63. W. La Barre, "Old and New World Narcotics: A Statistical Question and an Ethnological Reply," *Economic Botany* (1970), 24:73 – 80.

CHAPTER IV

Classical and Literary

The Greeks had two major and originally conflicting beliefs concerning the location of the life-force or soul: the *phrenes* and the *psyche*. The *phrenes*, or midriff, was clearly associated with breath *(pneuma)*, hence speech, thought, consciousness, life. The various states of breathing and the beating heart, especially under stress and emotion, were evidence for the *phrenes* location of the life of the individual. But to the Greeks the generative power of man was just as plainly in the head. As Onians writes,

It was natural and logical to think that the "life" or ψυχή issuing from a man must come from the "life" or ψυχή in him, from the head therefore, and, helping that location, to see in the seed, which causes the new life and which must have seemed the very stuff of life, a portion of the cerebrospinal substance in which was the life of the parent. It will indeed appear that this interpretation is vital to the whole thought.[1]

Hesiod relates sexual vigor to the seasons and the presence of moisture in the head, as does Alcaeus, and both are elucidated explicitly by Pliny.[2] The Homeric Hymn to the Pythian Apollo says that Zeus generated Athena specifically in his head *(gēinat' en koryphē)*, which Greeks took not metaphorically but with easy literality. Later in Greece the seed was *psyche* and stored in the head. Aristotle taught that the *psyche* is given in the seed of the male, which no doubt facilitated the widely held notion that a woman has no soul.[3] Pegasus, however, was engendered when the hero Perseus decapitated the Medusa (who was female); and Aphrodite sprang directly from the seafoam in Cyprus when the *mēdea* of Ouranos (not his head) were cut off by his son. The Pythagoreans and Orphics forbade eating beans, since these were assimilated to the heads of the parents.[4] The legend of the still-speaking severed head of Orpheus, that floated to Lesbos, came from the Danubian north, which, interestingly, was Celtic-speaking in Greek times. The head of Orpheus contained what was immortal, and thus alien Orphism and alien Pythagorism both agreed with Homer and the Olympianism with which these alien ideologies have usually been contrasted. Another interesting point is that in Orphic theogony bulls' heads were attached to the loins *(lagones)* of Phanes = Eros, who contained the seeds of all life.[5] The human head and the seed of grain are commonly juxtaposed in Greek metaphor: in one legend, Perseus cut off the Gorgon's head with a sickle.[6]

It seems curious to us that the Greeks did not associate the testes more especially with semen, since they were aware of the consequences of castration. But such was the potency of the prevailing concept of the psyche that eunuchs, they rationalized, commonly kept their head-hair (for all of the association of hair with virility) because of its growth so near the unconsumed *muelos* of the eunuch's brain, not because the supply of male hormones (which we know are implicated in baldness) had been cut off. And if eunuchs commonly became obese, this was plainly because of the accumulation of the unspent seed-equivalent, fat-*muelos*. Onians suggests that

the chief purpose originally behind the religious practice of self-castration was not, as has been thought, the bestowal of the seed-vessels wholesale upon some deity (see e.g., Frazer, *Golden Bough, Attis* I, pp. 268ff) or the loss of virility or the avoiding of defilement but the positive conservation of the seed, the life-stuff, the soul-stuff, with which the ψυχή was particularly identified.[7]

This interpretation is lent countenance by several elements in Greek thinking. In the first instance, the Greeks did not think the testes produced the seed. They were only a cache by the way, part of the channel, removal of which prevented issue. As late as Aristotle the testes were believed merely to retard the seed.[8] The continence-thesis of Onians also explains why, in Arnobius and Pausanias, Attis, being castrated, did not die in the ordinary way, his body did not corrupt, his hair continued to grow, and his little finger to move.[9] Onians' explanation also shows why, in the "Gospel to the Egyptians" quoted by Clement, the cessation of death depended on the cessation of procreation.[10] The Gnostics did not castrate or avoid coitus, but practiced "self-collection" of ψυχή, believing that thus they remained "virgin" (virility-laden).[11] Onians notes the analogy with plants of the ritual castration of Attis, since "for many plants to seed is to die." Reaping is thus decapitation. Meanwhile, the real self-castration ritual is not so much to give seed to the Magna Mater (which smacks of incest) as it is the abnegation of sexuality itself (which does not). Furthermore, the testes are not thought to be seed-producing, but their removal is thought to be seed-continent. Attis therefore seeks immortality, not incestuous union with the Great Mother.

Alcmaeon of Croton observed the connection of senses in the head with the brain, as evidenced by the "passages" he discovered from the eyes, etc., to the encephalon.[12] Alcmaeon was evidently an early anatomist, as well as experimentalist. However, against the commonly held belief in the exclusively *muelos* source of the seed, he held — as later did also Hippocrates, Democritus, and Diogenes of Apollonia — that *muelos* was gathered also from the flesh, more particularly from the fat, though to be sure gathered to the spinal marrow (as evidenced in spinal nerves) and thence to the brain; in this fashion might be explained why son resembles sire in appearance.

In the *Timaeus*, Plato replicates in classic source the popular Greek beliefs in *muelos*. The divine part of the marrow is in the head *(encephalos)*, and here life *(bios)* is ensconced. The psyche is itself seed *(sperma)*, or perhaps more precisely it is in the seed, and the seed is in the skull and in the spinal "generative marrow" and breathes through the genital.[13] The significance of breathing is important. The impregnation of Io by the *epipnoia* of Zeus is mentioned three times in Aeschylus; the seed is breath or *pneuma* for the stoics; and pro-creation as blowing is very explicit in Aristotle.[14] Indeed, the verb ψύχειν "to blow" is the nearest kin to ψυχή. The meaning is even in English: compare the "blow" of flies, a "by-blow" (for a bastard), and the various meanings of "blow" as orgasm. That the meaning is also Hindic suggests it may be pan – Indo-European, and allied with the *pneuma* concept of the soul.

The long-conflicting soul-sites of the Greeks *(phrenes* vs. *psyche)* are melded when brain and breath become united — yet still ex-pressing the ancient idea of *muelos* as brain – semen. The Pythago-rean Diogenes of Apollonia taught that "the seed is a drop of the brain containing in itself warm vapour (ἀτμός)," which vapor becomes in turn the psyche of the new creature. Thus far, birth; at the other end of life, death, a new fate awaits the cerebrospinal *muelos*. Greeks believed that both the genius of a man and his psyche might emerge from his loins as a snake when he died.[15] The great Hellenist Jane Ellen Harrison gives an abundance of examples of the soul-snake in Greek legend.[16] And like the psyche itself, the snake had the basic attribute of immortality.[17] But the essence of spirit in the bones was not lost either. Theseus was the most beloved of Athenian heroes, something of a rival of Heracles, the great Peloponnesian hero. The major place of worship of Theseus was east of the Agora in Athens, a large sanctuary to which Kimon brought the bones of Theseus from the island of Skyros in 476/5 B.C. Anciently, it was believed, spirit resides in the bones, a notion probably behind the later Christian use of saints' bones as miracle-cure relics. The earliest Greeks even knew the very old connection of male puberty with the sun. In his

Theogony, Hesiod mentions that the Lord Apollo brings young boys to manhood, with the aid of the nymph – daughters of Tethys and Ocean and their brothers the Rivers.[18]

However, the most dramatic archaism in all Greek thinking is the survival in Plato's fundamental philosophy of an Old Stone Age concept — a truly startling phenomenon for all that Plato was a notorious archaizer and reactionary through the influence upon him of Heraclitus, Pythagoras, and the old Orphic religion. Belief in the supernatural master-pattern of a species had been the first approximation of an answer to what later came to be called "the problem of the one and the many," of the universal and the particular, pattern and specimen, species and individual. Aristotle and later scientists were straightforward "nominalists" who saw the name as no more than an identifying linguistic tag; the name did not create the thing but was only a convenient way of classifying a specimen. But Plato transformed into an all-explanatory metaphysical principle the ancient mystical concept of the "master of animals," each *logos* or Word fathering its species.

The master of animals is a nearly worldwide belief of hunting peoples in an immortal spirit-principle provided for each animal species.[19] That is, the master is the divine pattern or *logos* of each particulated specimen or individual animal. The platonic *Idea* as father to each actuality is essentially the notion of Form as the master-of-animals father of each species of individual objects: the inseminating Idea of it is in the mind like metaphysical *muelos* and is the mystical progenitor of each material object. For Greeks the seminal Idea would as a matter of course be housed in the *psyche,* that is in the head, and (as so often in the history of thought) an implicit theory of the facts of life became a fundamental metaphysic. Indeed, the platonic Idea reverberated throughout the Great Tradition of subjective idealism in all later European philosophy and religion. The development of Platonism from this primitive conception is direct and demonstrable, though it need not detain us here.[20] The Great Tradition is, for our purposes at the moment, merely another example of the survival of the sexual superstition that concerns us here. Greeks also had the very archaic concept of the material finiteness of the male-stuff or *muelos*. A man aged because he had used up in venery his very soul- or life-substance. A boy became a man only after being *given muelos* — hence Greek love or *paiderastia*. And, finally, life could be preserved immortal only by self-containment, literal "continence" or ascetic non-spending of semen. Onians gives plentiful examples of the Greek rationale of aging, a matter of the drying-up of aiōn or *muelos*.[21] But the mythology of *paiderasiat* and asceticism requires further discussion.

One of the enduring puzzles in classic Greek culture is its institutionalized male homosexuality. Its origin is usually explained in that invading Dorian warriors were largely an all-male military society devoid of women. Yet the institution still flourished centuries later in settled classic times, was intimately connected with the education of boys, and was closely implicated with basic Greek rationalism.[22] Plato's *Symposium* is the famed apologia for the uranian *eros*, which, it was argued, is superior to common heterosexual *eros pandemos*. That male homosexuality was accepted socially among Greeks is shown, among many other indications, by the fact that even in the trial for his life, the openly discussed homosexuality of Socrates was not mentioned among the accusations (the crime of Socrates was political, i.e., treasonous alliance with the traditional enemies of Athens, namely Sparta and the Persians, which ended in the disastrous long Peloponnesian war and the destruction of Greek democracy).

The male-centered narcissism of their society doubtless played a part in Greek social structure and philosophy,[23] but there are deeper roots in the age-old sexual superstitions regarding *muelos*. The Danish psychiatrist Thorkil Vangaard writes that,

in the seventh century B.C., a Dorian nobleman through his phallus transferred to a boy the essence of his best qualities as a man. Since erotic pleasure was subordinated to a more important aim this was a genuinely symbolic act, the aim being to make of the boy a man with strength, a sense of duty, eloquence, cleverness, generosity, courage, and all the other noble virtues. Again, the act was not symbolic in the sense that we use the word, to denote something which seems to be what in reality is not. For the Dorian, a real event took place; through the paiderastic act the grown man's valuable qualities, which were as these people saw it incorporated in his phallus [more precisely in his semen], were transferred to the boy. With the help of Apollo the older man could convey his noble manhood to the youth. [24]

According to the Thera inscription, Crimon had connection with the son of Bathycles as a sacred act in the temple of Apollo himself, and in this fashion passed on his *aretē* to the boy. [25] The boy's name is not given, only that of his father, as testifying to a noble line capable of aspiring to *aretē*. The distinguished philologist E. Bethe has noted specifically that it is the semen of a man administered to the boy *per anum* which is the bearer of his *aretē*. [26] The qualities of *aretē* and character in a man's *psyche* are thus literally and materially given to the boy in the man's *muelos*.

Ephorus wrote in the fourth century B.C. that in Crete the elaborate formalities and sacrifices in arranging a paiderastic relationship were like those in an actual marriage — even to the costly custom in Crete and Thebes of the *erastes* giving the youth, *erómenos*, a suit of armor. [27] The emphasis on nobility and *aretē* gives us an understanding of why lawgivers like Solon forbade *paiderastia* to slaves as something absurd, for they had only their inferior qualities to pass on; and why a boy would be scorned if he chose a merely wealthy lover in lieu of a poor but noble one. Special respect was paid in public to a youth with a noble lover. Athenaeus wrote that "even great poets like Aeschylus and Sophocles introduced such themes of love on the stage in their tragedies — first that of Achilles and Patroclus, then that of the boys in Niobe." [28] Vangaard is at pains to show

that paiderasty was cultivated by heterosexually normal men in ancient Greece, where it did not presuppose an inversely homosexual type of personality. It was not considered a transgression, to be tolerated, nor was it felt to betoken any laxity in moral standards; it was a natural part of the lifestyle of the best of men, reflected in the stories of the gods and heroes of the people… in the Dorian world paiderasty was a central factor in the upbringing of boys and youths; it was a means of imparting to them the best qualities of the Dorian nobleman.[29]

From outside, from *muelos* housed in the head in the *psyche*-semen, the virtue (virility) of a man was passed on to a worthy youth. As in Asmat fellation, so in Doric pederasty; and a human or bull head laid on the groin would foment the same potency. Too, the lord Sun is patron of this male mystery.

If the psyche-semen is finite in quantity, then it behooves a man who seeks long life or immortality to conserve his life-substance, that is, not to "spend" his head-stuff (literally "capital"). For the classic peoples, "continence" was a literal matter. E. R. Dodds cites Aristoxenes and Iamblichus on sexual restraint; Diogenes Laertius, Diodorus, and Plutarch all considered sexual relations harmful; Hippolytus quotes Empedocles on the metaphysical ill effects of intercourse; and Strabo quotes Posidonius on the celibacy of holy men among the Thracian Getae.[30] Especially to be deplored is mere pleasure with courtesans beyond lawful necessary procreation. The usual Latin phrase is *caput limare cum aliqua (aliquo)*, "to wear away (file, rasp, gnaw) one's head with someone." Onians gives references from Livius Andronicus, Plautus, Juvenal, Festus, Propertius, Petronius, Terence, and Varro alluding to the concept.[31]

The Indo-European *diew*, descended to the Greeks as Zeus, means literally only "the shining one." Nineteenth-century scholars argued inconclusively whether the shining one was the sun, the moon, or the over-arching sky. Indo-European comparisons, especially from Sanskrit, would seem to indicate that "the shining one" is a figure of speech that should be taken literally. It can refer to the sun (or moon), the sky, the divine planets, lightning, Soma, light, life, and fire, as simply manifestations of the same phenomenon: the divine light. It is the male mystery: the life-soul.

To accept the meaning as literal is to find many things explained — all the way from why gods appear in an aura of light, a nimbus, or a halo, to why a visible flame hovered in battle above the head of the Homeric hero Diomede (and why El Greco still painted a candle-like flame over the head of each of twelve figures in his *Pentecost* about 1600).[32] The *aretē* of Ares is like fire in his head, which is why the redheaded woodpecker is his tutelary bird.[33] Zeus hurls fire in the lightning, and his thunderstone (a flint hand-axe) can still produce a spark of latent fire when struck; and it was fire that the culture-hero Prometheus stole from heaven.[34] (Like the All-Father Zeus, Eurasiatic – American shamans who control the spirits, and who like him are sometimes masters of animals, were invariably masters of fire and could juggle live coals.[35] Fire is the spirit the shaman ma-nipulates: the shaman who, fundamentally, controls the weather and the spirits of animals and men in all instances is in ancient thought *controlling fire*.[36]

In fact, fire is perhaps the most common form the divine mystery takes. The life of all creatures is fire; fire is the earthly form of heavenly light.[37] Impregnation by fire is a common idea.[38] The phallic Shiva, Pasupati, inseminating Master of Animals, carries a flame in one hand. Indeed, Vedic Agni (Latin *ignis*, "fire") *is* the sacrificial fire. One of his names is *Hiranyagarbhi* ("spark") the Golden Germ, the Child of Fire.[39] Agni is likened to lightning and to sexual orgasm, and discharges his seed as a sky-bull.[40] He is the guardian of Soma, the sacred mind-bending mushroom, which is specifically regarded as phallic.[41] In several passages in Sanskrit, Agni is even the Thun-derbird, an immensely ancient Eurasiatic – American concept — so old that it is also African.[42]

A striking assimilation of bones – *muelos* – fire – life is found in a pre-Buddhist *saitō goma* cult, in which "the ninety-one pieces of wood used to construct the fire are likened to the same number of bones in the human body — the burning fire signifies becoming a human being in the process of growth within the womb."[43] Again, "Self-generation, perpetual regeneration, has its image in Agni, the Fire" — for which reason a "perpetual fire" is a favorite symbol for immortality, commonly of a great hero.[44] In this context, fire is often associated with another very old symbol of life, in the red-ochre burials dating from the Upper Paleolithic (Aurignacian – Magdalenian) in Eurasia, which also occur in America.[45] (The Paleolithic Sungir red-ochre burial in Russia had had a layer of live coals placed beneath it; the painting red of a side-recess at Altamira and another at Gargas "appear to mean the magic making of life deep in the earth, as though in the menstruous womb of a woman.")[46] Red – fire – blood is thus a very old association.

Fire was known to pithecanthropine Peking Man during the Mindel glaciation or slightly thereafter, but in Europe only much later, in the middle Acheulian and after the Riss. In Africa there is no indication that fire was used before the end of the Acheulian.[47] It has been considered that only a safe focal location for females and young could allow the absence of protective males during the hunt, in the "trimorphous" hominization of man – woman — child among humans.[48] Oakley, indeed, has argued that "there is reason to believe that it was only when man had fire regularly at his disposal that he was able to compete successfully with carnivores in gaining occupation of habitable caves.[49] In both cases, fire is seen by these anthropologists as being of critical importance in the biological evolution of mankind. There can be little doubt that the mystery of fire has made a very deep impression on man.

The striking of flint on flint, giving so-called triboluminescence, has no fire-making properties. But sparks struck with flint and iron pyrites ("fool's gold") are hotly incendiary particles that easily ignite dry punk. The oldest evidence for this method of fire-making is Lower Paleolithic, the Mousterian of Arcy-sur-Cure; and abraded pyrite nodules are also found in Upper Paleolithic and Mesolithic sites.[50] The method used in ancient Greece, Italy, and China, this lasted in western Europe until the nineteenth century. The necessary differentness of flint and pyrites may relate to sexual metaphor.

The association of fire-making with sexual intercourse is well-nigh universal, especially with regard to the method of rubbing sticks together.[51] In the *Avesta*, one of the five sacred fires is found in the bodies of men and animals, following "a primitive theory of the fiery nature of the vital fluid or sap which runs through the entire scale of beings."[52] Many practices reveal the sexual metaphor. In India the sacred fire is kindled at weddings and becomes god of the house.[53] In Siberia, the Yakut have a "master" and the Orochi a "mistress of fire" whom they worship; but to prevent bad luck, fire must be kept within the clan and is related to getting game in the hunt.[54]

Heraclitus considered fire the fundamental cosmic reality and the life-giving seminal substance (πῦρ ἀεὶ ζωόν). Heraclitus was probably influenced by the Iranian dualism of darkness and light, and his views in turn certainly influenced Plato's concept of the *Idea* and thence the Stoic *logos*. God's creative Word in Genesis, *fiat lux*, like Heraclitean physics, may also be ultimately related to the Iranian cosmology. In any case, for Heraclitus, sacred seminal fire is the substrate of all changing reality. All fire flies upward, striving to rejoin the cosmic fire in the Empyrean.

The peoples of classic antiquity still had the association of sexuality with fire. Love is "fire in the bones" (and indeed the marrow "burns" in other emotions as well), which is not surprising inasmuch as marrow is thought to be the source of the seed.[55] Even more striking is the legend in Pliny that Servius Tullius was begotten by a phallus of fire that appeared on the hearth — much as Alexander the Great was reputed to have been begotten similarly by a serpent.[56] Latin writers perpetuated Greek doctrines: Pliny also wrote that the marrow descends through the vertebrae from the brain (*a cerebro medulla descendente*) and argued that brain-marrow is of the same substance as semen.[57] (Note that *cerebrum* is derived from Latin *creare*, "to create," and *sapere* "to know" means to have native juice.)

Romans, preoccupied with power, seem especially to emphasize that a man's strength is in his seed. Note the repeated reference in Livius Andronicus to "diminish one's head" with a courtesan.[58] *Venus enervat vires*, says the Latin Anthology; and even more generally everyone knew that *Post coitum animal triste*.[59] Lucretius wrote that men consume their strength *(adsumant vires)* and ultimately die of venery *(pereuntque labore)*, which in this sober writer had best be taken literally.[60] But these notions did not originate with the Romans. Precedents appear in Greece.

Hesiod seems to imply that the strength is in the liquid there, which is also the seed. He and other early poets characterize sexual love as 'loosing the limbs' (λυσιμελής) and, as biologist, Aristotle observed that 'the enfeebling ('loosing, relaxing,' ἔκλυσις) consequent upon issuing of even very little of the seed is conspicuous.' That the strength is in the seed and has its source in the source of the latter seems to be implied by the Latin use of *vires* and *virus* (cf. *vir*).... The result [of seminal emission] is 'lack of strength' (ἀδυναμια) and conversely where there is lack of strength there is lack of seed.[61]

This conclusion — it must be explicitly stated — rests on a complex of hoary superstitions about sexuality: that the supply of seminal fluid is concrete and limited; that procreative life-stuff and conscious-ness are the same substance; that the seed resides in the skull (and that hormone-secreting interstitial cells are the same as spermatozoa-producing ones).

There are other unfortunate indiscriminations. Marrow and fat are not sharply distinguished in classical thinking. Since both easily burn, they are regarded as obviously rich in hidden fire, life. The confounding of *muelos* and fat and their identification with seed and life explain the many associations of fat with sacred fire and light. A lighted candle is a small simulacrum of the eternal fire of the sun and of the hero's godlike immortality. A candle, as we shall in a moment see, is both a sacrifice and a prayer (beeswax, of course, is included with other fats).[62] The meaning of *anointment* is literal for the ancients: it is an en-oiling of the king or other favored individual, bestowing new life and strength. And, naturally, anointment is of his head.

Ever since the gloomy farmer-poet Hesiod, men have been puzzled as to why they got the tasty flesh of the sacrificial victim, while the gods got the fat and the bones.[63] This was not a trick of Prometheus, however, for in the famous story Zeus clearly knew which pile was which. Actually, nothing is more logical than that spirits should be fed spirit-food. The gods are not being cheated, but are getting the stuff of life. The sacrifice to them of fat and bones therefore keeps immortal gods immortal. In fact, Wellhausen wrote that "with the Hebrews, as with the whole ancient world, sacrifice constituted the main part of worship."[64]

We now have to deal with an animal once not only sacred, but sacred to the high god. It is a complex and ambivalent history. But instead of gratuitously contriving his own sophistic rationalizations and reinterpretations as to why other peoples *really* did what they did, the paleophilologist (like the anthropologist in general) does best to follow closely the old symbolisms provided by the "natives" themselves, mistaken as these seem to us. The associations are plentiful enough, even with a later-tabooed animal, and we may trace these associations on three continents. The pig was tabooed as a food not because the wise men secretly knew it provides excess cholesterol (this year's etiological myth), and not because of danger from trichina infestation (last year's myth: the sacred sources fail to specify not eating *uncooked* pork, for cooking easily kills trichina organisms).

The pig became tabooed, rather, because it had been the totemic animal of an earlier rival religion, that of the Magna Mater.[65] The association of the pig with the Great Mother in Greece is Neolithic (e.g., the pre-Hellenic Vinča civilization), and in Asia Minor was part of a pre-Hebraic goddess-worshiping religion of Semitic peoples. That the conflict was with a markedly patriarchal religion seems verified again, much later, in the history of Islam, which virtually extinguished a pig-raising culture that had once extended over north Africa from Egypt to the Canary Islands.[66] In Greece, the Olympian gods of the Indo-European invaders melded with earlier ones; but in Greco-Hebraic Christianity the Mother did not return until medieval and modern mariolatry.

The pig is highly suitable for symbolizing the great goddess, whose worship in Europe perhaps reached back to the hypermammalian "Venuses" of the Upper Paleolithic.[67] The pig, rich in fat, is notably fecund; note the root *fe- also in *fetus, femina, femur, feminis*. Classic peoples understood that pigs' fatness and fecundity (in their eyes much the same thing) resulted directly from their feeding on the "mast" (*mas*, male) of the oak, the All-Father's tree with its abundant replication of the glans or acorn (oak-kernel). Again, according to Frazer, the "reason why the Druids worshiped the mistletoe-bearing oak, above all the other trees in the forest, was the belief that every such oak had not only been struck by lightning but bore among its branches a visible emanation of the celestial fire."[68]

As to the potent male pig or boar, his name, *verres*, is related to *ver, vis, vir*, (Shakespeare's "full-acorned boar" is an especially complex pun, since the boar thus has a full glans and is also fat with *muelos* from having eaten acorns, as well as possessing conspicuous *glandes*).[69] The wild boar, no doubt because of his aggressiveness in attack, was the emblem not only of the war god of the Iron Age Celts, but also of the Twentieth Legion of Caesar's Romans who fought the latter-day Celtic Gauls.[70] The boar element figures in many Celtic names of both gods and men; the boar is also the consort of the Scandinavian Venus, Freya.[71] Several Homeric helmets made of boars' tusks can be found in Greek museums, and the boar's head or images of it formed a favorite Germanic headdress.

With its sharp tushes, the wild boar is a formidable animal, and hunting it has given men dangerous excitement from remote times. The Remigia cave (La Gasulla) shows a prehistoric boar hunt by men on foot.[72] In the multiple Levalloiso–Mousterian burial of Mt. Carmel Man in Israel, "the only object directly related to the skeletons was a wild boar mandible in the arms of Skūhl V."[73] Sculptures of pigs dating from every period in the Neolithic, in number equal to those of dogs, bulls, and he-goats, are known in all parts of Europe, where (as in Asia Minor) the pig was in special association with the vegetation goddess, or even represented the lady herself. An early Vinča vegetation goddess wears a pig mask; several Cucuteni pig sculptures have impressions of grain on them, quite like those on the clay goddess figures, in both cases probably for fomenting magic fertility of the crop. Two clay vessels found at the bottom of a Thuringian lake, one of them shaped like a boar and having bronze eyes, the other with three boars' heads, seem to be a proliferation of the same motif of fertility.[74] The mound of Nea Makri in central Greece contained sculptures of entire pigs; a beautiful head of Vinča period was found in Macedonia; and another early example came from a Starčevo settlement in northeastern Yugoslavia — all representative of the sacred animal of the goddess.[75] There are some indications that the great goddess was herself represented as a great sow in pre-Helladic "Pelasgian" Greece; and, in the late revival of the ancient Eleusinian Mysteries, a piglet was carried by each communicant in the ritual pilgrimage.

Hunting wild pigs is as prominent in classic legend as hunting the wild aurochs bull. The hero Theseus killed the great sow Phaia in Megara, bested the wild bull on the plain of Marathon, and joined with Pirithoos, King of the Lapiths, in the Calydonian boar hunt; Plutarch has him also hunting the wild sow of Crommyon. Adonis made love to the dread mother, for which, appropriately, he was killed by a wild boar. As hunter-goddess or Mistress of Animals, she could be murderously vengeful: "Œneus omitted Artemis when he made offerings to the rest of the gods, and she sent a wild boar to lay waste his rich orchards and vineyards; in the hunt for this boar a cumulation of woe arose from the anger of the offended goddess, which led to a destructive war."[76] In the midst of the high adventures of Jason and the Argonauts, en route to Colchis seeking gold, Apollonius considers it worthwhile to describe at length the death (predicted by fate) of one Idomon, son of Abas, from a wild boar's wounding him on the thigh.[77]

The hunt is prominent also in art. A Lycian tomb now in Istanbul shows on one side a lion hunt, on the other a boar hunt; a Scythian gold casting depicts a spirited boar hunt from horseback with bow and arrow; a silver dish, a Sasanian king on a boar hunt; a Safavid period miniature, a boar-hunting scene. Nor is the boar lacking in northern Europe. From Great Connell Abbey, in County Kildare, comes a ceramic bearing in impressed lines the figure of a wild boar feeding on acorns; the boar from Houndslow is a Celtic work of the British Bronze Age; and the Pictish slate carving from Knocknagael, Inverness-shire, reminds us that the boar was sacred to the Celts from the Early Iron Age onward.[78] "One of England's most treasured relics is a ninth-century ornament two and a half inches long known as the Alfred Jewel. Around its outer rim is the inscription 'Alfred ordered me made.' The rim, which terminates in a boar's head, encircles an enamel portrait of a king holding crossed sceptres."[79] It is believed that this jewel belonged to Britain's half-legendary king.

Feasting on the boar figures in Irish legends, especially since the champion's portion was often in dispute (Diodorus, Athenaeus, and Irish stories of Bricriu's Feast and of MacDatho's Pig).[80] The head of the boar, sacred to the fertility goddess Freyr (Freja) whose emblem it was, constituted the chief feature of the Yule feast; the combination of head, boar, and goddess indicates that this solstitial sun rite of Yule was a fertility festival before it became Christmas.[81] As to the boar hunt itself, it kept high significance well into the Renaissance. Burckhardt, citing the fourteenth-century historian Bernabò, writes that "the most important public object was the prince's boar-hunting; whoever interfered with it was put to death by torture; the terrified people were forced to maintain 5,000 boar hounds, with strict responsibility for their health and safety."[82] Other aristocrats elsewhere paralleled the Visconti princes of Milan in following the prestigeful boar hunt.

Because of the great importance of swine in the Neolithic of Europe, Asia Minor, and North Africa, the later taboo on pork presents something of a problem. Much of this history in fact may have happened outside the Semitic ambience. In Sumer, the pig had seemingly been the most kosher of animals, since it is the most frequently mentioned in the proverbs as being slaughtered for food.[83] The pig was probably first domesticated not at Jarmo or Jericho but at some other place, probably central Europe, perhaps about 6500 B.C., thus even earlier than were cattle.[84] (Indeed, a separate domestication of swine, like that of cattle, occurred in the Orient, whence the almost cultic position of the pig in Melanesia.)

As noted, the pig was a cult animal in much of Europe and Asia Minor, and in north Africa it was important in the Neolithic from Egypt to the Canary Islands. The pig "held a very important place in early Egypt but came to be considered unclean and fell into disrepute sometime after the Middle Kingdom. Subsequently the Arabs, with their even more extreme taboo against pork, practically obliterated the pig throughout North Africa," except among the Nuba, who are still mainly pagan and have continued the Neolithic pig culture into modern times.[85] Pig culture was probably important among the pre-Islamic Europeanoid Berber, and it survived in the Canary Island Guanche, among the Nuba, and in the Senegambian tribes of formerly Portuguese Guinea. The heterodox Moslem Zekara still eat pork; so do the Zaer and (surreptitiously) the Rif; the wild pig, as we have seen, is still hunted by such African tribes in the Ngulu.[86] The taboo on pork is properly a problem for the Egyptologist and need not detain us here.

Fat, fire, and fertility have now been fully discussed in terms of the pig, a symbolism that largely antedated the Indo-Europeans in Greece and Rome, who had yet another important symbol for divinity: gold. Classic peoples, in fact, came to contrive a network of mutually equivalent symbols for their divinely Shining One. Gold, which does not corrode or tarnish, is a fit symbol for the eternal undying "spiritual" male principle of life. "Incorruptible" gold plainly has eternal life. It is as immortal as the sun, which gold also symbolizes. The sun seems to die daily when it sinks into the mother earth at night, her son—consort, but is reborn each dawn, the Roman Sol Invictus. The Golden Bough on the oak, the parasitic mistletoe, is a memento of the sacred tree's having been struck by the divine fire of Zeus's lightning; and golden Apollo the Sun is appropriately Master of Animals, soul of the species, eternity of Pattern. Because of the seemingly infinite extensibility of gold leaf — like Fire, like *Logos* — the Orphics found gold symbolic of the soul and its immortality.[87] Another symbol for immortality was a spring of everflowing water — ever since Plautus the source of a river, incidentally, is its "head" — and Ponce de Leon was still seeking Orphic gold and the Fountain of Youth in Florida.[88] And in the immutable caste system of Plato's eternal authoritarian *Republic,* the rulers were "golden." Gold is as sacredly eternal as the Sun, as life itself.

Among the Jews, the injunction to "be fruitful and multiply" might seem to indicate an absence of antisexual feelings. There is also the bridegroom "coming out of his chamber [who] rejoiceth as a strong man to run a race" (Psalms 19:5). Indeed, says a remarkable Talmudic passage, in the next world "men would be called to account for the lawful pleasures which they refused in this life."[89] And yet, the Fall of Adam and Eve and their expulsion from the Garden (Genesis 2:17 – 3:19) was a direct consequence of sexual behavior. Jews are not wholly lacking in guilt over sexuality.[90] According to Talmudic and Kabbalist tradition, "every act of impurity, whether conscious or unconscious, engenders demons."[91] (Although commonly misinterpreted, the sin of Onan was refusal of levirate responsibilities toward his deceased brother's wife, not unlawful emission of seed as such.)

Greeks, we have noted, believed that at death a man's spinal marrow emerged from his loins in the form of a serpent.[92] The snake is a very old symbol of immortality because it seems to be reborn at each shedding of its skin. The Old Testament is full of references to the phallic snake and its immortality, but biblical Hebrews sought this boon most literally. In its context, the Mosaic story is quite clear: in the wilderness, many men were dying of snakebite, so practical Zipporah sought to make Moses akin to the snake that sloughs its skin. It was a direct apotropaic act. Whatever additional unconscious or secondary motivations or fortuitously achieved results there were, this was Zipporah's motive for circumcision.[93] That Moses in Egypt and in the Wilderness alike seems to have been a snake shaman, even before setting up the serpent-idol Nehushtam, adds further nuance to this meaning; and although Mosaic Egypt was in the full Bronze Age — indeed on the border of the Kenite Iron Age — the specified use of a flint knife betokens great antiquity for the practice.[94] And "la resurrezion della carne" is a far older trope than Boccaccio; that flaccid flesh becomes seeming bone could be another Stone Age metaphor.[95]

Later Jews had a special form of the ageless bone-engendering-life motif. Rabbinic tradition held that the *luz*, or lower coccyx end of the spine, remains in the grave after the rest of the body is gone and, when the dew of heaven falls on it, will become again a complete body and live.[96] Similarly, Jewish legend has it that the bones, nails, and brain come from the father, but flesh and blood from the mother—in good Old Stone Age tradition.[97] And seemingly before any influence from Europe, Hebrews and other Semites took and kept severed trophy heads in the belief they could prophesy.[98] Gold as a symbol of immortality was also Hebraic: in the Tabernacle, besides the brazen altar symbolic of the body was one of gold, which corresponded to the soul.[99] Gold lives forever, like the soul.

A most dramatic Old Stone Age survival, however, is in Scripture itself, in the resurrection of whole bodies from their bones. Ezekiel, in trance, was taken to the valley of bones where at the Lord's behest he performed like a paleolithic Master of Animals, summoning bones from their graves. In his words,

there was a noise, and behold a shaking, and the bones came together, bone to his bone.
And when I beheld, lo, the sinews and the flesh came up upon them, and the skin covered them above; but there was no breath in them (Ezekiel 37:7 – 8)

The prophet was then commanded to address the wind, and he did so, "and the breath came into them, and they lived, and stood up upon their feet, an exceeding great army (Ezekiel 37:10)." More had never been done with bones by the mightiest shamans of Old Stone Age hunters.

A rapid survey of the possible pan – Indo-European status of any symbolism is afforded by comparing classic Greek and Latin with Sanskrit sources. Here Vedantic Hinduism abundantly confirms nearly all the classic symbol-equations elicited above — if anything, even more explicitly. The symbolisms are, however, intricately inter-knit and redundant. Perhaps as good an entry as any into the complex of Hindu symbolism is afforded by an important ceremony, that of making the "Mahavira Vessel." The ritually made pot, the Mahavira Vessel, represents the decapitated head of the cosmic giant, Makha the Sun (who is also Vishnu the Preserver), restored in the sacred mystery of the hallucinogenic mushroom, Soma. Whereas the Greek gods were rendered immortal by imbibing *nectar* — probably honey-beer or "mead," a term that is linguistically pan – Indo-European — and *ambrosia*, the Brahmin priests themselves became living gods by eating the cognate to ambrosia, *amrita* or the ancient north-Eurasiatic hallucinogenic mushroom, *Amanita muscaria*.[100]

The vital sap that flowed from the head penetrated heaven and earth and mid-air, all that lies under the sun. The vital sap that flowed from the beheaded body was pressed out from it by Indra's might. Indra's might is sustained by Soma. In the transport caused by that drink of immortality the inspired poets sing about Indra's deeds.[101]

The oldest recording, in fact, of any Indo-European language is the Sanskrit poetic praise of Soma in the *Rig Veda*, dating from about 1500 B.C., the oldest portions of which may be as old in oral form as 1800 B.C. After the Aryan entry into India through the Hindu Kush, the Brahmins lost knowledge of the sacred plant, which does not grow south of the Himalayas. For millennia the identity of Soma was a puzzle for Hindu Vedantists, and for European scholars who have known Sanskrit since the eighteenth century — until Gordon Wasson had the brilliant insight to take literally the ecstatic Vedic apostrophes to Soma and found them to be recognizable botanical descriptions of *Amanita muscaria,* a narcotic mushroom still in use among Siberian tribes in modern centuries.

The 'All-encompassing Hero,' the 'Head of Makha,' the vessel that contains all life, that is flame, glow, and heat is the Sun. Mahavira is 'Lord of all the Worlds, Lord of all mind, Lord of all speech, Lord of all *tapas* (the fiery strength of asceticism), Lord of all brahman (the power of the sacred word), Lord of creatures, spirit of poets.'... The vessel is the member, milk is the semen, ejaculation — while boiling — into the fire as the divine womb, the birthplace of the gods, as generation.... The concept of the ascending, not ejaculated but transubstantiated, semen as the substance of illumination is the sustaining belief or experience that conjoins the shapes of the phallus and the head.[102]

The *tapas,* or ascetic practices (including sexual abstinence or continence), *engender* divine heat and enlightenment. Semen and brain are inextricably linked. Likewise,

"the vessel now stands for the linga. Head and procreative organ are coterminous yet do not overlap in the vision of the Brahmanas. Through long stretches of Indian thought and imagery, the symbolism of linga and head combined in the creation of a visual whole. The Mukhalinga of Siva, the phallus with a head or heads, is a concretely realized sculptural form perduring for two thousand years of Indian art."[103]

But this figure is not simply the psychiatrically familiar "body as penis" fantasy — though the sacred Ganges does in folk belief flow from the top of Siva's head, like water from the lingam. Semen must be saved, and sublimated from the lowest (sexual) lotus position in the pelvis to the highest sixth-lotus position, in the head. This is the goal of yoga.

There is another explicit linkage in Vedantism to a predecessor — divinity, betokening very great antiquity.

Agni's seed fell and became gold [Taittirīya Brāhmana I.1.3.8] and the seed of Siva, the source of Kūmara, is gold. By the time of the Epic (Mahabharata), Siva was also given the original Vedic epithet, "the golden womb," together with the golden seed [Linga I.20.80 – 86].... But another text describes the situation in reverse, maintaining that when Agni bore Siva's seed for 5,000 years (before the birth of Kūmara) his body became entirely golden, and so Agni became known as the bearer of the golden seed [Vāmana 57.9 – 10]. In fact, both Siva and Agni derive this property from the Vedic Prajāpati... [who] made it into all the animals [Tāṇḍya Mahābrāhmaṇa 8.2.10].[104]

Prajapati is the pre-Aryan "Master of Animals" of the prehistoric Mohenjo – Daran culture of northwestern India. The Hindu god Siva is the usual inheritor of this ancient title. Siva and his worshippers are often smeared with ashes. "Rebirth from fire is a generally accepted theme in Hinduism, and ashes are a particularly potent form of seed. The ashes of Kama (the Hindu Eros), when smeared upon Siva's body in place of the usual funeral ashes, arouse great desire.[105] Unfortunately, however the principle of "limited good" prevails, even for a god. The dilemma of Siva the *lingam* is that, although he may store up immense potency through *tapas,* the *apsaras* or heavenly maidens entice him from his semen-making meditations and he spends his power in venery. When this has occurred,

Siva must wander as a Kāpālika with a skull in his right hand to replenish the powers lost by making love to Pārvatī [Vamana 60.6]. The *tapas* which thus restores Siva also leads eventually into the next cycle of erotic activity; when Siva has married Pārvatī he carries her into the bedroom "with powers made great by his meditation" [Kumarasambhava 8.81], powers specifically said to be "an abundance of the qualities to achieve sexual intercourse" [Mallinatha's commentary on the above].... Both Siva's sexuality and his chastity pose certain threats to the balance of the universe: his *tapas* generates great heat which menaces the world, like the *tapas* of an ascetic, until an *apsaras* (Pārvatī) is sent by Indra to disperse it.... In Hindu terms, chastity builds up powers of *tapas* which are dissipated by sexual activity and then must be restored. When Siva's chastity becomes extreme, he must be seduced by Pārvatī and Kāma, only to become excessively sexual and forced by the gods and Agni to become chaste again.... *Tapas* and *kāma,* interchangeable forms of cosmic heat, replace and limit one another to maintain the balance of the universe.[106]

It is interesting that a skull is requisite to replenish the sexual energy of the Mukhalinga himself. For the skull is the source of seed.

Indian symbolic equations replicate the classic European ones. For the Hindus, gold was the stuff of life or immortality.[107] Gold is fire, gold is the seed of Agni = Fire, or of Indra, the god who fertilizes with lightning in the thunderstorm.[108] (And thunder, both in the Old World and in Mesoamerica, is the engender of mushrooms, including Soma-*Amanita* and psilocybin-*teonanácatl,* flesh of the gods—which is not surprising, given that the Thunderbird-eagle who produces lightning is a concept that spans three continents.)[109] In the Vedic horse sacrifice, its seed leaves it and becomes gold.[110] "The sacrificer places gold—the symbol of seed—in his mouth to avoid losing his true seed (and losing his own virile powers) during the night spent [abstinent] with his favorite wife."[111] (Hindus also believe there can be power-transmission from husband to lover via adulterous coitus, much in the same manner of power-transfer among Blackfoot Indians.)[112] "In the "*Taittirīya Saṃhita,* Agni, as he who burns, is described as the generative organ," not unlike the Roman phallus of fire.[113] Another logical symbol-equivalent need not be inferred, since one of the Upanishads states explicitly that Soma is the stallion's seed. "Semen *(retas)* has a secondary, metaphorical use as applied to the fructifying rain from heaven, the seed of the clouds. The flames of Agni are kindled by the seeds of heaven, and the Soma oblation into the fire is regarded as a seed."[114]

One of the *Purana* tales relates that two wives of a king had sexual intercourse, one "in the manner of a man," but the child of the other, since it was "born without male semen," lacked bones, and was a mere ball of flesh. "This is the natural consequence of the mating of females," states the modern Hindu editor.[115]

In the Indic area, males are often anxious about their virility. Inability to have an erection may be remedied by drinking the semen of another man, "which will expand the semen-carrying ducts" (Susruta 3.2.18).[116] (This practice also occurs in Tantric rituals.)[117] In modern Sri Lanka, a Singhalese anthropologist tells us that "many young unmarried men, particularly students in the university dormitories, eat raw eggs in the morning to enhance strength... to compensate for the loss of vitality due to night emissions, masturbation, or an imagined discharge of semen in the urine. In Sri Lanka the term for egg is *biju,* which is also used for seed, semen, and penis."[118] Thus, "to eat seed in order to produce seed is a simple homeopathic method that makes sense in Western terms too," remarks the Sanskritist commentator. According to another anthropologist, Carstairs,

It is significant that, in addition to milk, rice, and eggs, butter is regarded as a producer of semen; bridegrooms and other male guests at weddings are encouraged to swallow as much as two pounds of ghee at a single sitting, a feat regarded 'as a mark of virility.... And the boasting and teasing which attend these feasts make it clear that ghi is being equated with semen.' The Vedic equivalent of butter and semen on the ritual and mythic level is thus put to use on the medical and psychological level.[119]

Indeed, this replenishment is directly needed, for the uses of marriage are dangerous to the male, since the female exhausts him of his life.

Hindu asceticism derives immediately from its believers' cosmo-physiological fantasies about sexuality. "The direct equation of semen with life emerges from the medical texts, where semen is expressly said to promote longevity; therefore, to live long, one must retain semen (Caraka I.25.39). This is merely a reformulation of the Vedic hypothesis: Soma promotes immortality: to become immortal, one must drink Soma."[120] The Upanishads teach that "a man's power, *šakti,* enters him in food and is stored in semen: to increase and retain this *šakti,* males must retain their semen and hence lead an ascetic life."[121] The medical textbooks are quite specific about the process. It takes sixty drops of blood to make one drop of semen. There are seven *dhatus* or stages of the refinement process of which semen is the product. In one day only twenty drops of semen are made, but a single orgasm loses about fifty drops. In a man's lifetime only four pints altogether can be made, and when this amount is gone, the man may either die or live like a vegetable. Understandably, the Upanishads regard coitus as a form of death. Loss of manhood even in manly acts is loss of life.

Hinduism is replete with metaphors for the destructive rapaciousness of the female. In love talk, "I will take away your life's breath" means stealing the semen (Devibhāgavata Purana 5.10.32–34; 5.11.19 –21, 25–77); in a South Indian myth a Brahmin wife decapitates her husband (and, not to leave this merely symbolic, cuts off his phallus as well); the Goddess decapitates and with another "mouth" devours her consort — indeed, Kali is sometimes represented as a spider — and "every actual sexual act, is by implication, a fatal battle."[122] The love-death is not mere metaphor: a Baiga myth tells how death first came into the world, with sexual intercourse.[123] Hindus have ways of avoiding loss, by practicing coitus interruptus or through magic formulas that return seed to the male. In other situations,

the man who spills his semen is instructed to place it between his breasts or eyebrows (Bṛhadaraṇyaka Upaniṣad 6.4.4–5). These two places are the two most important cakras or centers through which, in Kundalini Yoga, the seed moves upward from the base of the spine to the tip of the head. The rich supply of semen stored in the yogi's head is symbolized by the high-piled hair... in the "snake locks" or matted hair, that characterize the Sadhu.[124]

The middle of the forehead may represent a displacement upward of the female organ. "The yogi, by drawing his semen to this special point, the site of the third eye, reverses the flow of normal sexuality and hence the flow of normal time; thus he transmutes seed into Soma, converting the fatal act of intercourse into an internalized act that will assure immortality."[125] The head as "the reservoir in which semen is stored" is the rationale behind the belief that "there are some holy men who learn the trick of stopping the falling nectar [from the brain, down the uvula] with their tongues; and as long as they do that, they cannot die... [A powerful yogi is said to have an] intact store of rich, uncurdled semen in his head."[126]

These are not arcane doctrines but popular beliefs. "Although the yogic aspiration to transmute semen into Soma is taken literally, and acted upon, by only a small and esoteric section of Indian society, it is known and subscribed to on a theoretical level by most Indians, even illiterate villagers."[127] Ancient physiological notions are thus widespread, however erroneous. Sakhya yoga, for example, teaches that there is

a great vein of the body running up the spinal column. This vein, called the *sushumna,* contain[s] six 'wheels' *(chakras)* or concentrations of psychic energy at different points along its length, [the lowest being the male *kundalini* 'serpent power'].... The serpent power should be awakened by yogic exercises and rise up the spinal vein, passing through all the wheels of psychic force to unite with the topmost lotus. By arousing this serpent power the yogi hoped to gain spiritual energy and uniting it with the highest lotus was thought to bring him salvation, though many yogis practiced this arousal for the sake of supernatural powers rather than salvation [to immortality].[128]

Tantra, of which this is an example, comprises various non-Vedic Hindu and Buddhist sects that worship divinities concerned with sexual energy, often called sects "of the left hand" being secret and taboo-breaking, or because the female *šakti* or sexual energy sat to the god's left. Shiva and Krishna, incidentally, are both non-Vedic deities, and Tantrism emerged in highly popular movements in the early centuries of our era evidently from very old Asiatic sources, since both Tibetan *bon* and pre-Confucian popular Chinese Taoism share features with Tantrism.

Taoists taught not only *coitus reservatus* by mental discipline, but by physical methods. Ejaculation was prevented by pressing the seminal duct with the fingers, thus diverting the fluid into the bladder. But Taoist theory, like Indian Yogic and Tantric, held that the semen *(ching)* would 'flow upwards' along the spinal column to 'nourish the brain' and the entire system.[129]

Inasmuch as the brain – semen fantasy is not only European and Indic and also archaic Chinese, it might appear old enough to have influenced the earliest inhabitants of Southeast and insular Asia as well, as part of a primordial paleolithic culture. And since headhunting is as old in China as Peking Man (and as old in Europe as other Neanderthaloids), headhunting ideology might well have influenced the oldest culture of *Homo sapiens* in Melanesia, Indonesia, and the Americas.

Notes

1. R. B. Onians, *The Origins of European Thought* (New York: Arno Press, 1973), pp. 109–10.

2. Hesiod, *Works and Days*, ll. 586 – 87, in H. G. Evelyn-White, ed., *Hesiod: The Homeric Hymns and Homerica* (New York: Putnam, 1929), pp. 46–47. For the engendering of Athena, Hesiod, *Theogony*, l. 924, in Evelyn-White, *ibid.*, pp. 146–47, and *Homeric Hymn to Athena*, ll. 4–5, Evelyn-White, *ibid.*, pp. 454–55; Alcaeus, Fragment, 39, 6–7 (Bgk.); Pliny, *Natural History*, xxii, 22, 86. For *Hymn to Pythian Apollo*, Onians, *Origins*, p. 111.

3. Aristotle, *De generatione animalium*, 737a, 30ff; cf. Aeschylus, *Eumenides*, 658 – 66; H. Diels, *Die Fragmente der Vorsokratiker*, W. Krantz, ed., 2 vols. (Dublin and Zurich: Weidman, 1966) 1:4; Diels, *The Pre-Socratic Philosophers* Kathleen Freeman, trans., (Oxford: Blackwell, 1948). Pegasus and the Medusa, Ovid, *Fasti*, 451.

4. Diogenes Laertius, *Lives of Eminent Philosophers*, 2 vols. (New York: Putnam, 1925), 2:355 – 57; Onians, *Origins*, p. 112 n. 2. For the bean, favism, and Indo-European totemism, W. La Barre, *The Human Animal* (Chicago: University of Chicago Press, 1954), p. 356, and W. La Barre, *The Ghost Dance* (New York: Doubleday, 1970), pp. 510–11 n. 50.

5. Fragment, 54 (Kern).

6. Onians, *Origins*, p. 114 n. 5.

7. Onians, *Origins*, p. 110 n. 1.

8. Aristotle, *De generatione animalium*, A, 717a, 20ff; cf. Aristotle, *Problemata*, 879b, 897b, 23ff.

9. Arnobius, *adv. Nat.*, v, 7; Pausanias, *Description of Greece*, vii, 17; cf. Homer, *Iliad*, xix, 24ff; see Onians, *Origins*, p. 110 n. 1.

10. Clement, *Strom.*, III, 13, 92.

11. Epiphan., *Panar.*, I, 2, 26, 9; II, 15.

12. Diels, *Fragmente*, A, 5, 8, 10, 11. See also T. Gomperz, *Greek Thinking: A History of Ancient Philosophy*, 4 vols. (London: Murray, 1901 – 1912), 1:148. For Hippocrates, Democritus, and Diogenes of Apollonia, see Onians, *Origins*, p. 115. Cf. Pindar, *Pythian Odes*, 80ff.

13. Plato, *Timaeus*, 91B; cf. 73F, 77D, 85B ff., 91A f.

14. Aristotle, *Historia animalium*, 586a, 15f; Aristotle, *De generatione animalium*, 728a, 9f, 736b, 33ff; Aristotle, *Problemata*, 879b, 1ff, 880a, 30. For English "blow," see Eric Partridge, *A Dictionary of Slang and Unconventional English*, 3d ed. (New York: Macmillan, 1949). For the Pythagorean Diogenes of Apollonia, Diels, *Fragmente*, 1:13.

15. Pliny, *Natural History*, Book X, lxxxvi, 188, H. Rackham, trans., 10 vols. (Cambridge: Harvard University Press, 1940), 3:411 – 13, but cf. 3:515. Onians, *Origins*, pp. 129, 206, 232; La Barre, *The Ghost Dance*, pp. 36, 455 – 57, cf. pp. 415, 424, 435 – 36, 438, 462 – 63, 466, 542; for Semitic parallels, pp. 193 n. 32, 561 – 62, 564 – 67. Robert Briffault's, *The Mothers: A Study of the Origins of Sentiments and Institutions*, 3 vols. (London: Macmillan, 1927; New York: Johnson Reprint Corporation, 1969) has a chapter on snakes and immortality, 2:641 – 51, ch. 21. "Pythagoras says: 'serpents are created out of the spinal marrow of corpses' — a thing which Ovid also calls to mind in the books of the Metamorphoses, when he says, 'Some there are who believe that sealed in the grave, the spine rotting, marrows of humankind do turn themselves into serpents.'" T. H. White, ed., *The Bestiary: A Book of Beasts* (New York: Putnam, Capricorn Books, 1960), pp. 190 – 91.

16. Jane Ellen Harrison, *Prolegomena to the Study of Greek Religion*, 2d ed. (Cambridge: At the University Press, 1908), passim.

17. Weston La Barre, *They Shall Take Up Serpents: Psychology of the Southern Snakehandling Cult* (Minneapolis: University of Minnesota Press, 1962), pp. 77 – 85, 172.

18. Hesiod, *Theogony*, 63.

19. La Barre, *Ghost Dance*, pp. 163 – 65, 189 – 91.

20. La Barre, *Ghost Dance*, pp. 541, 547.

21. Onians, *Origins*, pp. 214 – 15, 219 – 21; pp. 205 – 6, 208 on *aiōn* = *muelos*.

22. La Barre, *Ghost Dance*, pp. 446, 489 – 93, 497, 530.

23. La Barre, *Ghost Dance*, pp. 446 – 47, 498, 540.

24. Thorkil Vangaard, *Phallós: A Symbol and Its History in the Male World* (New York: International Universities Press, 1972), p. 12. More specifically, the phallos is only the conduit of the *psyche*, for the *muelos* is the semen.

25. La Barre, *Human Animal*, p. 325; cf. pp. 311, 329, 332.

26. E. Bethe, "Die Dorische Knabenliebe, ihre Ethik und ihre Idee," *Rheinisches Museum für Philologie*, new series, (1907) 62:438 – 75. George Devereux also has qualifications to make concerning the pathic quality of Greek *paiderastia* ("Greek Pseudo-Homosexuality," *Symbolae Osloenses* [1967], 42:69 – 92); the present discussion supports both Bethe and Devereux. See also Hans Kelsen, "Platonic Love," *American Imago* (1942), 3 (1 – 2):3 – 110; on *muelos*, p. 58 n. 2.

27. Strabo, 10, 4, 21, citing Ephorus.

28. Athenaeus, XIII, 601 a.

29. Vangaard, *Phallós*, p. 32.

30. E. R. Dodds, *The Greeks and the Irrational* (Berkeley: University of California Press, 1951), p. 175 n. 122. Aristoxenes, Fr. 39W; Iamblichus, *Life of Pythagoras*, 132, 209ff; Diogenes Laertius, 8.9; Diodorus 10.9.3ff; Plutarch, *Quaestiones Cons.*, 3.6.3, 654b; Strabo, 7.3.3f; cf. Lucretius, *De Rerum Natura*, iv, 1121.

31. Onians, *Origins*, pp. 123 – 24.

32. La Barre, *Ghost Dance*, pp. 442 – 43; André Bonnard, *Greek Civilization from the Iliad to the Parthenon*, 3 vols. (London: George Allen & Unwin, 1937), 1:38 – 39.

33. La Barre, *Ghost Dance*, pp. 461 – 62. The ecstatic dancers in Euripides "carried fire on their heads and it did not burn them" (*Bacchae* 757); but this seems, rather, a miraculous or magical act, to be compared with shamanistic fire- or snakehandling. See E. R. Dodds, *The Greeks and the Irrational* (Berkeley: University of California Press, 1951), Appendix I, Maenadism, p. 274.

34. La Barre, *Ghost Dance*, pp. 453 – 54. The obscure epithet *latiaris* for Jupiter in the feretory handax *(silex)* in his ancient temple in the Alban Hills south of Rome may now be understood as *fire* (or lightning) "hidden" in the flint.

35. La Barre, *Ghost Dance*, pp. 138, 178, 440; M. Eliade, *Forgerons et alchemistes* (Paris: Flammarion, 1956), pp. 81ff.

36. Dodds, *Greeks and the Irrational*, pp. 298 – 99; Carl-Martin Edsman, *Ignis divinus: Le feu comme moyen de rajeunissement et d'immortalité* (Lund, Sweden: Skrifter utgivna av Vetenskap-Societeten i. Lund, 34, 1949); and Gaston Bachelard, *Le psychanalyse de feu* (Paris: Gallimard, 1935). Cf M. G. Levin and L. P. Potapov, *The Peoples of Siberia*, (Chicago: University of Chicago Press, 1964), pp. 281, 756.

37. A. E. Crawley, "Fire, firegods," in J. Hastings, ed., *Encyclopedia of Religion and Ethics*, ("*Hastings Encyclopedia*"), 13 vols. (New York: Scribner, 1908 – 1926), 6:26 – 30.

38. A. E. Crawley, *The Mystic Rose* (London: Methuen, 1902), p. 197; J. G. Frazer, *Totemism and Exogamy*, 4 vols. (London: Macmillan, 1910), 2:258ff.

39. Stella Kramrisch, "The Triple Structure of Creation in the R̥g Veda," *History of Religions* (1962), 2:140 – 75, p. 142.

40. Kramrisch, "Triple Structure," pp. 162, 168 n. 3, 170 n. 38, 174.

41. Kramrisch, "Triple Structure," p. 172; La Barre, *Culture in Context*, (Durham, N.C.: Duke University Press, 1980), pp. 108 – 15; La Barre, *Ghost Dance*, pp. 158 – 60; cf. pp. 144 – 45, 178, 194, 454, 468 n. 7.

42. Kramrisch, "Triple Structure," p. 171; cf. La Barre, *Ghost Dance*, pp. 148, 176, 193, 195; T. O. Beidelman, "Swazi Royal Ritual," *Africa*, (1966), 36:373–405, p. 387. Gelele, king of Dahomey, in Richard Burton's presence, "refreshed himself by drinking rum from brass-mounted skulls of former enemy chiefs." Byron Farwell, *Burton: A Biography of Sir Richard Francis Burton* (New York: Holt, Rinehart & Winston, 1964) p. 234, cf. p. 237. Africa has other elements of *muelos* mythology, but these are not impressive compared to the northern hemisphere Paleolithic and New World Mesolithic, and are ignored here.

43. H. Byron Earhart, "Four Ritual Periods of Haguro Shugandō in Northeastern Japan," *History of Religions* (1965), 5:93–113, p. 111.

44. Kramrisch, "Triple Structure," p. 142.

45. La Barre, *Ghost Dance*, pp. 347, 407–9; J. B. Griffin, "Some Prehistoric Connections Between Siberia and America," in J. R. Caldwell, ed., *New Roads to Yesterday: Essays in Archaeology*, pp. 277–301, (New York: Basic Books, 1966), p. 291.

46. La Barre, *Ghost Dance*, p. 395, cf. p. 347; and pp. 407–9, where many examples are given.

47. P. Oakley, "Use of Fire by Neanderthal Man and His Precursors," in G. H. R. von Koenigswald, ed., *Hundert Jahre Neanderthaler 1856–1956*, pp. 267–69 (Utrecht, Netherlands: Kominck en Zoon, 1958), p. 267.

48. W. La Barre, Foreword to Melford Spiro, *Gender and Culture: Kibbutz Women Revisited* (Durham, N.C.: Duke University Press, 1979), pp. viii–xi; La Barre, *Ghost Dance*, pp. 73–89; La Barre, "Anthropological Perspectives on Sexuality," in D. Grummon and A. H. Barclay, eds., *Sexuality: A Search for Perspective*, pp. 38–53 (New York: Van Nostrand Reinhold, 1971).

49. Quoted from Oakley, "Use of Fire," p. 267; but for fuller treatment see his "Fire as Palaeolithic Tool and Weapon," *Proceedings of the Prehistorians Society*, (1956), n.s. 21:36–48.

50. Oakley, "Use of Fire," p. 268.

51. E.g., Bantu, Beidelman, *Swazi Social Structure*, p. 390.

52. Jacques Duchesne-Guillemin, "Heraclitus and Iran," *History of Religions* (1963), 3:34–39, pp. 38–39.

53. Crawley, "Fire, firegods," pp. 27, 29.

54. Levin and Potapov, *Peoples of Siberia*, pp. 287, 356, 820.

55. Propertius, III (IV), 17, 9, in Onians, *Origins*, p. 152; cf. Ovid, *Amoris* III, x, 29f; *Metamorphoses* IX, 485; XIV, 351; *Ars Amatoria* III, 793.

56. Pliny, *Natural History*, XXXVI, 27, 204; cf. Ovid, *Fasti*, VI, 631, in Onians, *Origins*, p. 158.

57. Pliny, *Natural History*, XI, 37, 178; cf. Macrobius, VII, 9, 22; from Onians, *Origins*, p. 149.

58. Onians, *Origins*, pp. 123–24.

59. *Anthologia Latina sive Poesis Latinae*, Franz Buecheler and Alexander Riese, eds., 2 vols in 5 parts (Leipzig: Tuebner, 1884), 633, 3.

60. Lucretius, *De Rerum Natura*, IV, 1121.

61. Hesiod, *Theogony*, 910; Aristotle, *De generatione animalium*, 725b, 6f, and 17–21, in Onians, *Origins*, p. 187 and n. 7; ct. p. 175.

62. Beeswax, Onians, *Origins*, p. 238 n. 1; anointment, pp. 188–89. In the baptism of witches, the chrism is actual human seed. M. A. Murray, *The Witch-Cult in Western Europe* (Oxford: Clarendon Press, 1921), pp. 247–48. A. E. Crawley has a chapter on "The Practice and Psychology of Anointment, with Special Reference to the Hindus," in *Studies in Savages and Sex* (New York: Dutton, 1926), pp. 187–218.

63. Hesiod, *Theogony* 535ff; Onians, *Origins*, p. 279. Chemical analysis has ascertained that the white pigment used in the Lascaux Cave paintings was made of calcium phosphate from calcined animal bones. (A. Leroi-Gourhan, "The Archaeology of Lascaux Cave," *Scientific American* (June 1982), 246 (6):104–112, p. 110. It is difficult to avoid the inference that *bone dust gave life* to the animals portrayed.

64. J. Wellhausen, *Prolegomena to the History of Ancient Israel* (New York: Meridian, 1957), pp. 52, 56, 63–64, 67, 78. (First translated into English in 1885.)

65. La Barre, *Ghost Dance*, pp. 392–93, 399–400, 442, 542–44, 597 n. 29, 604.

66. G. P. Murdock, *Africa* (New York: McGraw-Hill, 1959), pp. 116, 266–67; survival in Canaries, p. 19; Ngulu, T. O. Beidelman, "Pig *(Guluwe)*: An Essay on Ngulu Sexual Symbolism," *Southwestern Journal of Anthropology* (1964), 20:359–92, p. 371.

67. La Barre, *Ghost Dance*, pp. 399–400, 424 n. 14, 425–27.

68. J. G. Frazer, *Baldur the Beautiful*, 2 vols. (London: Macmillan, 1923), ii, 301. Annual observations, made for seventeen years in the Lippe-Detmold forest, showed that lightning-stricken oaks exceeded the number of stricken beeches by 60 to 1. Warde Fowler, "The Oak and the Thunder God," *Archiv für Religionswissenschaft* (1913), 16:318. I thank Professor Derek Freeman for this reference.

69. Eric Partridge, *Shakespeare's Bawdy* (New York: Dutton, 1955), p. 156, on *Cymbeline*, II, v, 15 – 18; Jane Renfrew, *Palaeoethnobotany* (London: Methuen, 1973), ch. 17, pp. 154ff. Ancient Hebrews called testes into witness in oaths; Homeric Greeks used swine in taking oaths by the older gods and those of the underworld (A. G. Keller, *Homeric Society: A Sociological Study of the Iliad and the Odyssey* [London: Longmans, Green, 1902], p. 130). The soothsayer Calchas sacrificed a boar when Agamemnon was about to depart for Troy, and each man swore enmity to Priam in its blood (Demosthenes, *Orations*, xxiii). Compare Pausanias on swearing on the flesh of a boar (Pausanias, iii, 20, 9; iv, 15, 8; v, 24, 9). See also Onians, *Origins*, p. 155, on acorns and pigs.

70. Irwin Isenberg, "Caesar," *American Heritage*, 1964, pictured pp. 79, 91.

71. Grimm's *Deutsche Mythologie*, p. 139, cited in R. P. Knight and T. Wright, *Sexual Symbolism: A History of Phallic Worship* (New York: Julian Press, 1957), p. 27.

72. J. B. Porcar, "Impresiones sobre el Arte Rupestre Existente en el Maeztrago," in L. P. García and E. R. Parelló, eds., *Prehistoric Art of the Western Mediterranean and the Sahara*, pp. 159 – 66. Viking Fund Publications in Anthropology no. 39 (New York, 1964), fig. 1, p. 163.

73. Michael H. Day, *Guide to Fossil Man: A Handbook of Human Palaeontology* (New York: World, 1965), p. 90. My colleague Matt Cartmill tells me of the Arthurian legend of Culhweh and Olwen in the *Mabinogion*: "Hunting of the magical boar Twrch Trwyth to pluck magical instruments from its head, which permit a ritual decapitation of a giant and allow the hero to marry the giant's daughter."

74. Maringer, *Gods of Prehistoric Man*, p. 150.

75. F. C. Sillar and R. M. Meyler, *The Symbolic Pig: An Anthology of Pigs in Literature and Art* (Edinburgh: Oliver & Boyd, 1961); T. G. E. Powell, *Prehistoric Art* (New York: Praeger, 1966), figs. 262, 263.

76. Keller, *Homeric Society*, p. 135.

77. Apollonius, *The Voyage of Argo*, E. V. Rieu, trans. (Baltimore: Penguin 1959).

78. M. Rostovtzeff, *The Animal Style in South Russia and China* (Princeton, N.J.: Princeton University Press, 1929), pl. XVI, 2. Freer Gallery, Washington: Sasanian, 34.23; Safavid, 54.32; Dublin, National Museum, 64, 5-1, 8. N. K. Chadwick, *Celtic Britain* (New York: Prager, 1963), fig. 27, p. 130; T. G. E. Powell, *The Celts*, (New York: Praeger, 1958) pl. 5d, pp. 256 – 57, 266, 270, 272.

79. F. R. Donovan, *The Vikings*, (New York, Harper & Row, 1964) p. 45, pictured.

80. Powell, *The Celts*, p. 111.

81. Onians, *Origins*, p. 126 n.5. Cf. Tacitus, *Germania*, 45 (Peterson, ed., p. 239).

82. J. J. Burckhardt, *Civilization of the Renaissance in Italy* (New York: Macmillan, 1948), p. 13.

83. S. N. Kramer, *History Begins at Sumer* (New York: Anchor Books, 1959), p. 134.

84. Wolf Herre, "The Science and History of Domestic Animals," in D. Brothwell and E. Higgs, eds., *Science and Archaeology*, pp. 235 – 49 (New York: Basic Books, 1963), pp. 242 – 43. See also F. E. Zeuner, *A History of Domesticated Animals* (London: Hutchinson, 1963), pp. 258 – 64.

85. Murdock, *Africa*, p. 165; cf. pp. 105, 266 – 67.

86. Murdock, *Africa*, pp. 19, 116.

87. La Barre, *Ghost Dance*, p. 509 n. 44.

88. Onians, *Origins*, pp. 125, 231; Ethel King, *The Fountain of Youth and Ponce de Leon* (Brooklyn: Gaus, 1963).

89. *Hastings Encyclopedia*, 8:40, citing *Kiddushim*, ch. 4.

90. For suggested psychodynamic reasons for Jewish relative freedom from antisexuality see La Barre, *Ghost Dance*, p. 604. See also Onians, *Origins*, p. 110 n.

91. G. G. Scholem, *On the Kabbalah and its Symbolism* (New York: Schocken, 1970), p. 155.

92. Harrison, *Prolegomena*, pp. 234 – 37, 325 – 31; M. P. Nilsson, *The Minoan – Mycenaean Religion and Its Survival in Greek Religion* (Lund, Sweden: C. W. K. Gleerup, 1950), p. 273f; Onians, *Origins*, p. 206 n. 5; La Barre, *Ghost Dance*, p. 455. "One is led to wonder whether the fascinating quality of the snake [in sloughing its skin] might not have contributed to the origin of circumcision. . . . Circumcision is an attempt to obtain for the penis the reinvigoration experienced by the snake, through a bit of sympathetic magic" — but Slater is discussing the *resurrezion della carne:* tumescence, not immortality. Philip Slater, *The Glory of Hera* (Boston: Beacon Press, 1966), pp. 84–85 n. 5.

93. La Barre, *They Shall Take Up Serpents*, pp. 78 – 80; La Barre, *Ghost Dance*, pp. 47, 559 – 61, 566, 580, 594 – 95 n. 12; V. Crapanzano, "Rites of Return: Circumcision in Morocco, " in Werner Muensterberger and L. Bryce Boyer, eds., *The Psychoanalytic Study of Society*, 9:15 – 36 (New York:

Psychohistory Press, 1980); R. B. Graber, "A Psychocultural Theory of Male Genital Mutilation," *Journal of Psychoanalytic Anthropology* (1981), 4(4):413 – 34. For Jewish legends concerning circumcision: Louis Ginsberg, *The Legends of the Jews* (New York: Simon and Schuster, 1961), pp. 109, 306, 323, 437. There are three inconsistent accounts of circumcision: Priestly (Abraham and the Covenant), Deuteronomic (Joshua, on entering Canaan), and Yahwist (Exodus 4). The last is probably the oldest, since Moses may have learned circumcision from the Egyptians.

94. La Barre, *Ghost Dance*, pp. 564 – 67.

95. Erich Auerbach, *Mimesis* (Princeton, N. J.: Princeton University Press, 1953), p. 225; cf. Gargantua's *ad te levari* in the same sense, p. 226.

96. Onians, *Origins*, p. 288; compare the Arabic *al Ajb* view of Moslems.

97. Ginsberg, *Legends*, p. 387.

98. Onians, *Origins*, p. 103 n. 3.

99. Ginsberg, *Legends*, pp. 412 – 13.

100. Mesolithic antiquity is argued for the ritual use of narcotic mushrooms in Eurasia and America (La Barre, *Ghost Dance*, p. 468 n. 7; see also pp. 158 – 59 n. 37, 435. For a précis of Gordon Wasson's identification of Soma, see La Barre, *Culture in Context*, pp. 108 – 115; first published in *American Anthropologist* (1970), 72:368 – 73.

101. Stella Kramrisch, "The Mahāvīra Vessel and the Plant Putika," *Journal of the American Oriental Society* (April – June 1975), 95(2):222 – 35, p. 226.

102. Kramrisch, "Mahāvīra Vessel," p. 230, 232.

103. Kramrisch, "Mahāvīra Vessel," p. 234.

104. Wendy Doniger O'Flaherty, "Asceticism and Sexuality in the Mythology of Siva, Part II," *History of Religions* (August 1969), 9(1):1 – 41, pp. 6 – 9. Note the Roman understanding that gold was used for crowns to represent fire, flame, divine energy, life (Onians, *Origins*, p. 165 n. 6); the emperor Gallienus not only wore rays to make his head shine but also sprinkled gold filings in his hair (Trebell., Vit. Gall. 16 in Onians, p. 166); compare the flame above the head of a Homeric hero such as Diomedes, and the Welch conceit that a candlelike flame preceded a corpse to its grave, and that a flame sometimes appeared above the womb of a pregnant woman.

105. O'Flaherty, "Asceticism," p. 19, citing Satapatha Brāhmana, Padma, Brahmānanda, Linga, and Siva Jñānosaṃhita.

106. O'Flaherty, "Asceticism," pp. 37 – 39.

107. Onians, *Origins*, p. 106, citing a number of passages in the Satapatha Brāhmana.

108. Onians, *Origins*, pp. 156, n. 2, 166; Satapatha Brāhmana 2.1.1.5, etc.

109. La Barre, *Ghost Dance*, pp. 454, 468 n. 7; Onians, *Origins*, p. 136 n. 2; Kramrisch, "Mahāvīra Vessel," p. 23; La Barre, *Ghost Dance*, pp. 195 n. 47, 435.

110. Wendy Doniger O'Flaherty, *Women, Androgynes, and Other Mythical Beasts* (Chicago: University of Chicago Press, 1980), p. 155.

111. Bandhāyana Šranta Sūtra, in O'Flaherty, *Women*, p. 159.

112. O'Flaherty, *Women*, p. 156; cf. p. 31 on semen-power transfer. A cuckold can also take magic revenge on his wife's lover and render him impotent by using symbolic arrows smeared with ghee. Brhadāranyaka Upanisad 6.4.12, in O'Flaherty, *Women*, p. 30.

113. Walter O. Kaelber, "*Tapas*, Birth, and Spiritual Rebirth in the Veda," *History of Religions* (May 1976), 15(4):343–85, p. 350. There are many more symbolisms in this author for the fire – life – semen – male principle. For the fire – gold – semen – Soma complex, see also M. Eliade, "Spirit, Light, and Seed," *History of Religions* (August 1971), 11(1):1 – 30. Eliade finds the South American Desana sun – light – sex – hallucinogen complex "a surprising parallel" (p. 25) to his Eurasiatic examples. In many motifs it is not so much parallel as identity in the arbitrary association of details. Fire – phallus, Taittirīya Saṃhitā, 1.5.9.1, in Kaelber, p. 350.

114. Soma as stallion-semen, Brhadāranyaka Upanisad, 1.1.1; Rig Veda, 1.164.36; Taittirīya Saṃhitā, 8.4.18, in O'Flaherty, *Women*, p. 21. Rain as semen, Soma-seed, Rig Veda,1.71.8; 5.17.3 (p. 20).

115. Padma Purana Svargakhanda 16.11 – 14, in O'Flaherty, *Women*, pp. 40 – 41; cf. p. 33. For Nilakantha's (1862) discussion of bones from the father and commentary on the lesbian-born child, see his edition of *Mahabharata* 12.293.16 – 17.

116. O'Flaherty, *Women*, p. 51. In the *bhakti* love-worship of Krishna, however, the transvestism of males is not explicitly homosexual: "The devotee visualizes himself as a woman not merely because god is male but because in the Hindu view the stance of the ideal devotee is identical with the stance of the ideal woman." O'Flaherty, *Women*, pp. 88 – 89.

117. O'Flaherty cites Tucci and Carstairs on Tantrism; the fluid drunk in the Kali skull-cup may be both semen and menstrual blood (p. 52). Disapprobated "yogis of the left hand" are accused of drinking urine also; a former Prime Minister confessed to this regimen for alleged health reasons.

118. Gananath Obeyesekere, quoted in O'Flaherty, *Women*, p. 51.

119. Carstairs, cited in O'Flaherty, *Women*, p. 51. On butter = semen, see also the *Mahabharata* 12.207, and O'Flaherty, *Women*, p. 47, citing Egnor.

120. O'Flaherty, *Women*, p. 44.

121. O'Flaherty, *Women*, on *šakti*, p. 45; *dhatu*, p. 36; loss of seed as a kind of death, p. 31.

122. O'Flaherty, *Women*, pp. 81, 83; cf. *Rig Veda* 1.179.4.

123. Carstairs, in O'Flaherty, *Women*, pp. 44; 137, citing Elwin.

124. O'Flaherty, *Women*, p. 45. Techniques for reclaiming semen from the woman in ordinary coitus are taught in the Bṛhadāraṇyaka Upaniṣad 6.4.10 and 4 – 5, in O'Flaherty, pp. 30 – 31.

125. Carstairs, quoted in O'Flaherty, *Women*, p. 46.

126. *Ibid.*

127. O'Flaherty, *Women*, p. 47.

128. Geoffrey Parrinder, *Sex in the World's Religions* (New York: Oxford University Press, 1980), p. 35.

129. Parrinder, *Sex in the World's Religions* p. 85; see also Holmes L. Welch, "The Bellagio Conference on Taoist Studies," *History of Religions* (November 1969 – February 1970), 9(2 – 3):107 – 36. The authority is E. R. van Gulik, *Sexual Life in Ancient China* (Leiden: Brill, 1961), pp. 46f, 65, 160ff. "The Arab practice of *Imsák*, the special art of delaying the male orgasm, is probably selfishly intended to decrease the loss of precious semen rather than altruistically increasing the sexual pleasure of females." Alan Dundes, "Wet and Dry, the Evil Eye: An Essay in Indo-European and Semitic Worldview," in *Interpreting Folklore*, pp. 93 – 133 (Bloomington: Indiana University Press, 1980), p. 60, citing *The Perfumed Garden of Shaykh Nefzawi*, Richard F. Burton, trans., A. H. Walton, ed., (London: Neville Spearman, 1963). On male "limited good," see John H. Weakland, "Orality in Chinese Conceptions of Male Genital Sexuality," *Psychiatry* (1956), 19:237 – 47; Leigh Minturn and John T. Hitchcock, *The Rajputs of Khalapur, India* (New York: Wiley, 1966) and the Andalusian saying, "Si quieres llegar a viejo, guarda la leche en el pellejo, [If you want to reach old age, keep your semen— literally, milk— inside your skin]" (recorded by the anthropologist Stanley Brandes in 1976).

CHAPTER V

Christianity, Renaissance, and the Victorians

Christianity is often charged with having invented a contorted anti-sexuality that like a pall gradually overshadowed a healthy and happy pagan naturalism. Admittedly, the contrast between Homeric and Hellenistic attitudes toward sexuality in Greece is considerably large. But the accusation against Christianity is unjust mainly because it is inaccurate historically. It is not that antisexuality is not deeply enmeshed in the Pauline New Testament, for it is, but rather that its sources lie earlier, most immediately in that most un-Greek of philosophers, Plato, and in the influence upon him of Heraclitus, Pythagoras, and the Egyptians. Heraclitus in turn was affected by Iranian dualism; and an archaizing Pythagorism merged as an influence with a revived Orphism, of mid-European origins, in later Hellenistic times of classic collapse. Certainly Eurasiatic Manichism, spanning twelve centuries from Spain to China, was older and wider than early Pauline Christianity. From within Greek philosophy itself, the Cynics and the Sophists made their contributions to a Hellenizing Paul as well.[1]

The institutionalization of Christian antisexuality is clear-cut in monasticism. In the Decian persecution, many Egyptian Christians removed to the wilderness as hermits (*eremos,* "desert"). (An irony overtook St. Simeon Stylites, seeking solitude on his pillar in the Syrian desert — and gradually becoming surrounded by impressionable imitators in a forest of pillars, until finally a church with four apses was built focusing upon him.) As the number of hermits in Egypt grew, they formed non-familial communes of cenobites (*koinos bios*, "life in common"). But there were earlier precedents for monasticism as well. One of the four Jewish sects of Jesus' time, the Essenes, lived a virtually monastic life; and the Pythagorans of Magna Graecia in southern Italy formed ritualized anticivilian and semi-religious brotherhoods. About A.D. 340, St. Pachomius founded nunneries for the *non nuptae*, unmarried women assembled in convent. Monasticism reached the West toward the end of the fourth century, and St. Benedict founded the model for monasteries at Monte Cassino with its famed scholarship and a work ethic much older than Protestantism.[2]

There were other gross antisexualities. Origen castrated himself, and so many Christians sought this same small price for immortality that surgeons were besieged with requests for the operation — a penal offense under Roman law which the government refused to sanction.[3] However, religious castration also had an earlier tradition in the pre-Judaic cults of the Magna Mater (and even survived in the Skoptzi of south Russia in modern times) so that it needed no encouragement from St. Paul.[4]

Although antisexuality did not originate with Christianity, it is pointless to deny the extent and tenacity of the hostility. The Platonic – Gnostic temper found physical reality essentially evil, the ideal male logos being everywhere contaminated with female materia; the mirror reality befouls the divine. Redemption is possible only in death itself, dissolving the dualism, separating pure spirit from gross matter, like Heraclitean fire flying upward to the empyrean. In the Platonic pun, *soma* is the *sema* of the *psyche*: "body" is the "prison" of the "soul." Consequently, active sexuality, which compounds and pollutes male ideality of pattern with female particularity and reality, is intrinsically evil. Platonic idealism is the eternal haven of the tender-minded, in an imperfect world.

The early Fathers of the Church are explicit in their body-hating Platonism. According to Irenaeus, both Saturninus and Basilides declared that marriage and generation are from Satan. Tatian called marriage corruption and fornication. Tertullian wrote that women are the gateway of hell, and *inter feces et urinam nascimur*. Ambrose and Jerome used equally extravagant language, and they seemed to tolerate marriage only because it produced virgins, though the highest type of adult Christian would have been celibate. Jovinian was excommunicated for denying what Augustine had asserted, that virginity was a state superior to marriage. The odd idea evolved that virgins are the brides of Christ, hence seduction of one is adultery as well — ignoring that the deity himself had been conceived in an identical situation.[5]

Even within marriage, intercourse should not be performed for pleasure, a dogma reasserted in a papal bull in the middle of the present century. The Church cut down the number of days on which even married couples might legitimately have intercourse. It was made illegal on Sundays, Wednesdays, and Fridays — the equivalent of five months in the year. Then it became illegal for forty days before Easter, forty days before Christmas, three days before attending Communion — despite rules requiring frequent attendance — and forty days after parturition. Additionally, of course, it was forbidden during penance.[6] Taylor believes the tabooing even of masturbation "increased the number of guilt-ridden personalities in society and produced that atmosphere of despair which marked the thirteenth and fourteenth centuries."[7] Intention was not the crux of the crime, fortifying the suspicion that orgasm itself was the disaster to life. "Involuntary nocturnal pollutions were a sin; the offender must rise at once and sing seven penitential psalms, with a further thirty in the morning. If the pollution occurred when he had fallen asleep in church, he must sing the whole psalter."[8]

The extravagance of Christian terror at any manifestation of sexuality — for it is manifest terror — is all the more striking because it is certainly not justified in the Jewish Old Testament tradition. Deeply rooted folk physiology concerning sex, prevalent since the Paleolithic, and its reinforcement by the intellectual detritus of ruined classic civilization are together requisite for an understanding. As Taylor says,

Only real desperation is enough to explain the ruthlessness with which the Church repeatedly distorted and even falsified the Biblical record in order to produce justification for its laws. For such extreme asceticism is not enjoined by the Bible, and certainly not by the New Testament. As Lecky shows, "The Fathers laid down as a distinct proposition that pious frauds were justifiable and even laudable," and he adds, "immediately, all ecclesiastical literature became tainted with a spirit of the most unblushing mendacity."[9]

But of course precedent for this too may be found in the "noble lie" of Plato.[10] Here, erroneous "facts of life," however ancient, ultimately require in their defense such tawdry jiggery-pokery and pious flummery. However, by recognizing the persistence of the hoary ideology, we can still attribute good intentions to the Church authorities. They were saving man from himself.

Nevertheless, as an ethical system Christianity was perhaps fatally poisoned by its indefatigable, obscene, and futile war against a most profound and necessary need — for the love, indeed, that it proclaimed central in its doctrine. Religion came to appear the implacable enemy of human nature itself — with the unanticipated result that, after a rediscovery in the Renaissance of part of our pagan past, modern man has largely abjured tradition as such as his primary touchstone for truth. Perhaps a gain; but also a loss. The contemporary mass loss of literacy even threatens to result in the loss of any past against which to revolt, or of a knowledge of alternatives to sort out for choice. It is possible, too, to castrate the mind.

The tenacity of ancient error, however — great age merely ensconces it still more obdurately and ineradicably — is truly astonishing. The *muelos* fantasy can still be documented in the full

Renaissance, though all I wish in this cursive essay is to show it persisting in the mainstream of our literature. Shakespeare's term for *muelos* is "marrow" and occurs several times in his works, as also does "tallow." Perhaps the most explicit reference is the most Shakespearean, when Parolles cries out to Bertram, who has just wedded Helena but refuses to bed her:

To th' wars, my boy, to th' wars!
He wears his honour in a box unseen,
That hugs his kicky-wicky here at home,
Spending his manly marrow in her arms,
Which should sustain the bound and high curvet
Of Mars's fiery steed.

> (*All's Well That Ends Well*, II, iii, 281 – 86)

Evidently virility is lost in virile acts; certainly love-making ruins a man for war.

Marrow-fat as ointment and sexual substance appears to be implicated in

Dry up thy marrows, vines, and plow-torn leas;
Whereof ungrateful man, with liquorish [lecherous] draughts
And morsels unctuous, greases his pure mind.

> (*Timon of Athens*, IV, iii, 194 – 95)

Mind and marrow are conjoined in the lines

Lust and liberty
Creep in the minds and marrows of our youth,
That 'gainst the stream of virtue they may strive;

> (*Timon of Athens*, IV, i, 25 – 27)

Partridge defines marrow here as "mettle, spunk, semen."[11] He says, "Mettle, 'natural adour,' as early as Shakespeare had the derivative sense, 'abundance (and vigour) of semen'; cf. the variant *spunk*. *Mettlesome* and *spunky*, besides meaning 'courageous,' 'high-spirited,' mean 'sexually vigorous or *ardent*,' (*Mettle* is a variant of *metal*; etymologically, *spunk* is 'tinder, or a spark.')"[12]

A direct metaphor of *mettle* that Elizabethans would recognize as semen is afforded by the angry apostrophe of the Dauphin:

> My faith and honour,
> Our madams mock at us, and plainly say
> Our mettle is bred out, and they will give
> Their bodies to the lust of English youth
> To new-store France with bastard warriors!
>
> (*Henry V*, III, v, 27 – 31)

Falstaff declares woefully

> I am here a Windsor stag, and the fattest, I think, i' th' forest—
> Send me a cool rut-time, Jove, or who can blame me to piss my tallow?
>
> (*Merry Wives of Windsor*, V, v, 13 – 16)

Partridge glosses "piss one's tallow" as "literally to lose weight by freely sweating [but here meaning] to be so sexually excited as to experience a seminal emission. Originally, hunting slang; its appositeness to Falstaff is clear — did he not 'lard the lean earth' with his sweat?"[13] Since physical excercise tends to reduce weight, sweat is evidently regarded as melted fat—which is further erroneous physiology. But so does sexuality presumably reduce fat:

> Thou wouldst have plunged thyself
> In general riot, melted down thy youth
> In different beds of lust,
> Dissolved thy marrow, thy youthly ardour, virility, strength
>
> (*Timon of Athens*, IV, iii, 225 – 57)

where "melt" (used of either sex) is a euphemism for orgasm, and doubles with the melting of fat, marrow, or tallow. In *Venus and Adonis,* love is referred to as

The marrow-eating sickness, whose attaint
Disorder breeds by heating of the blood. (741 – 42)

The *Oxford English Dictionary* (s.v. "marrow") notes that "In the 16th – 17th c love was often said to 'burn' or 'melt the marrow.'"

Tindale writes in 1530 unambiguously of "the pith, the quicke, the lyfe, the spirit, the marrow"; Fleming, in 1576, "If I were in the perle of my youth, and had in my bones marrow... I wold not." Spencer writes on lechery "that rotts the marrow and consumes the braine" (*Faerie Queen*, I, 4, 26); Kyd writes, in 1572, of "marrow-burning love" — a concept found in Shakespeare as

My flesh is soft, and plumpe, my marrow burning.

(*Venus and Adonis*, 192)

In 1602 *The Return from Parnassus* decries youth "spending the marrow of their flowering age" (IV, iii, 1935) — to be compared with Macbeth's cry to Banquo's ghost after the murder, "Thy bones are marrowless, thy blood is cold" (*Macbeth*, III, iv, 92), and (in another contemporary author), "O that marrowless age should stuffe the hollow bones with dambd desire." A writer in 1592 wonders that "such is the force of marrow-burning love." A fine classicist, Dryden in 1647 translated Virgil's *Georgics* (III, 428) as "When in the Spring's Approach Their Marrow Burns." There are variants: "Their marrow-boyling loves" (1598), and "That heart-swelting, Marrow-melting Fire" — and the motive is not obscure when (1555) "The bridegroom eateth to his supper... a little of the maribone of a Chamel" — which recalls Browning's hero:

He was fresh-sinewed every joint,
Each bone new-marrowed.

(*Sordello*, V, 500)

But marrow figures not only in poetry. Francis Bacon wrote soberly in 1626 that "The Skull hath Braines, as a kind of Marrow, within it. The Back Bone hath one Kinde of Marrow, which hath an affinity with the Braine" (*Sylvia*, 750). The eighteenth century retained the sense of marrow as seed. William Hamilton (1704 – 1754) exulted

Busk ye, busk ye, my bonny bonny bride,
Busk ye, busk ye, my winsome marrow.

The nineteenth century had not forgotten the traditional meanings. Samuel Woodworth warned a potential enemy in 1814, "Better not invade; Yankees have the marrow" (*The Patriotic Diggers,* stanza I), and in 1848 Lytton wrote of "the pith and marrow of manhood" (*Harold,* V, iii).

Tallow and marrow are synonymous for the manly *muelos.* But whereas "marrow" always retained a sense of dignity, "tallow" from Shakespeare onward often carried a taint of vulgarity:

Her rags and the tallow in them will burn a Poland winter.

(*Comedy of Errors,* III, i, 100)

Call me ribs, call me tallow

(*1 Henry IV,* II, iv, 125)

A wassail candle, my lord, all tallow

(*2 Henry IV,* I, ii, 179)

Unlustrous as the smoky light
That's fed with stinking tallow

(*Cymbelline,* I, vi, 110)

Thou whoreson, obscene, greasy tallow ketch

(*1 Henry IV,* II, iv, 252)

Out, you geen-sickness carrion, you baggage!
You tallow face.

(*Romeo and Juliet,* III, v, 158)

— a tone retained from Falstaff's vulgarity (*Merry Wives of Windsor,* V, v, 13 – 16) into Sir Richard Burton's "we are forty sharpers, who will piss our tallow into thy womb this night, from dusk to dawn."[14]

The designation of "sperm" for the spermaceti or fine fatty substance in the head of the sperm whale is certainly related to the *muelos* belief that the semen comes from the "marrow" in the head. The supposed connection of the sperm and spermaceti accounts for an alchemist's recipe of 1471, which says "use... Sperma Cete ana with redd Wyne when ye wax old,"[15] evidently for rejuvenation. A curious misinterpretation of the spouting of the whale dates from 1398: "The whale haþ gret plente of sperma, and after þat he gendreþ with þe female, superfluite þerof fleteþ aboue þe water."[16] In view of this notion, evidently the "blow hole" of a whale is thought to be concerned not wholly with breathing.

The sperm whale "was first described by Chisius in 1605 from specimens cast up on the coast of Holland in 1598 and 1601," but a satisfactory explanation of whale-spouting is still lacking.[17] The theory that visibility of the spout results from moisture condensing in cold air would not obtain in tropical climates; and the hypothesis that expended spermaceti contains dissolved nitrogen from the whale's blood in order to prevent the "bends" from prolonged diving, is ingenious but unproven; in any case, spermaceti expended through the "blowhole" implies orgasm. The largest of all animals ever, the blue whale is still largely unknown, and from man's rapacity may disappear before the answer is known.

Beyond the words of Shakespeare and others, we have graphic evidence that the belief in brain-*muelos* as the source of sperm persisted in the Renaissance. Leonardo da Vinci, Renaissance man par excellence, seems to have had some ambivalence about the genitals. In one of his Notebooks he wrote: "The act of procreation and the members employed therein are so repulsive, that were it not for the beauty of the faces and the adornments of the action and the pent-up impulse, nature would lose the human species."[18] In his discussion *Della Verga,* however, he is impressed by the apparent autonomy of the organ and is also critical of tradition: "It seems therefore that this creature has often a life and intelligence separate from the man, and it would appear that the man is in the wrong in being ashamed to give it a name or to exhibit it, seeking rather constantly to cover and conceal what he ought to adorn and display with ceremony as a ministrant."[19] Leonardo writes a bit poignantly, "would that it might please our Creator that I were able to read the nature of man and his customs even as I describe his figure!"[20]

Leonardo believed the tradition that spinal marrow is the same substance as the brain whence it is derived.[21] But there is reason to doubt that Leonardo's dissections ever included the male genitourinary system. Anatomical dissection would have resolved the evident conflict between classical authorities; but, instead, anatomy and embryology were altered to accommodate conflicting venerable traditions:

From Galen comes the belief that the sperm is derived from the testes, the "first cause" of man's existence; from Hippocrates through Avicenna comes the idea that the soul, the "second cause" of existence, is infused from the spinal cord, the site of the generative faculty. Consequently, the penis has two canals in the drawing—the upper conducting the animal spirit or soul, the latter allowing for passage of sperm and urine. [22]

The great scientist remained bound by the ancient superstition. "There are at least twelve coition studies in his anatomical drawings, certainly more than in any of our best textbooks in physiology, which shows that the inquiring mind did not stop at investigating that which in his personal life was taboo." [23] In at least one of his sagittal-section drawings, Leonardo clearly shows spinal ducts to the penis that do not exist. [24]

We have now to consider a curious trend in cultural history, a massive shift in psychological attitude. The classical attitude toward sexuality, largely revived in Leonardo's and Shakespeare's day, was at times bawdy, but hardly repressive. Classic Martial, for example, complains that his rich friend Candidus is so stingy that he would not lend him a male slave for sexual purposes, "but my own hand is Ganymede to serve me," and (as his lover Lygdus did not meet a tryst) "when I have lain fruitlessly racked with lingering desire, a substitute has often come to my rescue" — neither of which appears to betray anxiety about homosexuality or masturbation. [25] The attitude toward masturbation at least continued in the Renaissance. In the *Spiritual Exercises* of St. Ignatius Loyola (1491 – 1556), which so carefully discriminates between venial and mortal sins, masturbation is not mentioned. [26]

However, in *The Anatomy of Melancholy*, Burton exemplified in 1621 an old conjecture that is certainly a retrospective falsification of etymological history, in his term "manustupration," which derived from a supposed *manus* plus *stuprare*, "to defile by the hand." Cockeram employed the term again in 1623, and Stapleton is his translation of Juvenal. This editorializing etymology — resuscitated briefly in the Victorian era, but now obsolete as being completely erroneous — reveals more of then-current attitudes than it does of etymologically formative Latin times. The reconstructed analysis of this word "of obscure origin" accepted by the *Oxford English Dictionary* is that of Brugmann: "**mastiturbāri* f. **mazdo-* (cf. Gr. μέζεα pl). virile member + *turba* disturbance" — but perhaps more plausibly we have an alternative in Onians' *mas*, "a male person," or Partridge's "seed" plus *turbāri*, deponent of "to disturb" (the deponent allowing of passive or middle grammatical form but reflexive meaning). Thus, to masturbate is to interfere with a male, oneself or another, or to roil maleness.

The later mounting campaign against masturbation appears to have begun with the blatant misrepresentation of a biblical story, that of Onan (the Bible nowhere mentions, or even refers to masturbation as such).[27] Scholars are agreed that the "sin of Onan" was not his spilling seed upon the ground as such, but in so doing evidencing his refusal to "raise up seed" for his deceased brother with his widow, that is, shirking the traditional brotherly obligation of the levirate. The first literature on the new "onanism" — certainly first inasmuch as the author is responsible for coining the term in its erroneous meaning — is a pamphlet published anonymously in England about 1720 (soon republished and translated in several languages) by one Becker or Bekker, probably of Dutch origin, entitled *Onania, or the Heinous Sin of Self-Pollution and All its Frightful Consequences, in Both Sexes, Considered with Spiritual and Physical Advice to Those Who Have Already Injur'd Themselves by this Abominable Practice, to which is Subjoin'd a Letter from a Lady to the Author, Concerning the Use and Abuse of the Marriage Bed, with the Author's Reply.* The author declares that "the sin of Onan, and God's sudden vengeance upon it are so remarkable, that everybody will easily perceive, that from the name I have deriv'd the running Title of this little Book" — unfortunately a total misconstrual of Onan's act, which was at worst an attempt at birth control, not masturbation.

Gross theological error, however, did nothing to dampen the spread of this concept of "onanism" and its manifold evils. A Swiss physician, S. A. Tissot wrote *L'Onanisme: Dissertation sur les maladies produites par la masturbation* (1770), a quickly famous work which spread like wildfire in many reprintings and translations. Among numerous cases, Tissot mentions two men who indulged in excessive masturbation, one of whom became insane, and "the other dried out his brain so prodigiously that it could be heard rattling in his skull.[28] The theologian Jean-Philippe Dutoit-Mambrini, in his tract *De l'onanisme: ou discours philosophique et moral sur la luxure artificielle, et sur tous les crimes relatifs* (1760), bolstered Tissot's medical arguments with extensive tirades against lascivious dreams. In his three chapters on *des soilures de la nuit,* which he pronounced excusable and possibly even healthful, he inveighed against the nocturnal fantasies for which he held the dreamer fully responsible.[29] (Thus, for him, not seminal emission but pleasure was the evil.) In 1755, A. Hume wrote the similarly titled *Onanism; Or a Treatise upon Disorders produced by Masturbation.*

The semen-saving of Christian ascetics had had the practical goal of *salvation.* That is, soul-saving (life-saving) is equivalent to immortality achieved. However, a tradition as old as the thirteenth-century theologian Duns Scotus taught that semen too long hoarded turned into poison (hence Dutoit-Mambrini's view), producing giddiness and clouding of the eyesight.[30] In the article on "Onanie" in his *Dictionnaire philosophique* of 1764, that old scoffer and unbeliever Voltaire showed that he had missed neither Tissot's tract on *Onanie* nor Duns Scotus's opinion that excessive continence can be harmful. Voltaire wrote in mock bewilderment, "How then can we use the precious fluid which nature has given us to multiply the race? Scatter it round and it will kill you — store it up, and it will kill you just as surely."[31] Semen is apparently deadly stuff, wrote one commentator on this passage.

The appropriate scientific approach would seem to require study of two groups of controls, those who expended versus those who conserved semen. However, because of the potentially dire effects of either regime, the experiment could obviously not be made on human subjects. There is also an evidently insuperable Christian objection, put best by Ferreres, in his *Compendium Theologicae Moralis:* "The effusion of semen would be legitimate for medical purposes if only it could be achieved without causing pleasure."[32] Faced with this stricture, scientific inquiry on the matter must of necessity grind to a halt.

One eighteenth-century rationalist made a finer discrimination than most;

The depression which follows the emission of the spermatic fluid at least indicates to us that at this moment we are undergoing the loss of an extremely ardent and active liquid. Should we place the blame upon the loss of a small quantity of that marrowy, palpable juice that is contained in the seminal vesicles? Would the bodily organism, for which it was already as non-existent, immediately take note of the loss of such a humor? The answer is undoubtedly no. But it is not the same with the fiery substance of which we have only a certain amount and with which all the vital centers are in direct communication. Thus to lose flesh, marrow, juice and fluid is of little importance. To lose the fire, the seminal fire, that is the great sacrifice.[33]

One is taken aback that the ancient notion of fire-life in the seed should survive so vigorously and literally in the Age of Reason. But even accepting the old belief in the finiteness of the fluid, one is also puzzled why the supposed infinitude of fire would not serve to make replenishment.

Religious and moral qualms about the mortal effects of loss of semen grew in the following centuries into a veritable medical obsession with the supposed debilitating effects on mind and body. In

1708, Boerhaave expressed the consensus that "the rash expenditure of semen brings on a lassitude, a feebleness, a weakening of motion, fits, wasting, dryness, fevers, aching of the cerebral membranes, obscuring of the sense and above all the eyes, a decay of the spinal cord, a fatuity, and other like evils."[34] Doctors invented the malady "spermatorrhea" (also known as "involuntary leakage" or "the bachelor's disease"), leading to physical decay, probable insanity, and even possible death. Dr. Francis Lallemand in fact wrote three volumes on *Des pertes séminales involuntaires* (1836 – 1843).[35]

The fear gradually suffused the literature of the times in all European languages, though it sometimes took secondary symbolic forms:

The idea that moral delinquency, especially masturbation, leads to weakness of the spine is extremely widespread. On the first page of Zschokke's *Die Zauberin Sidonia*, written in 1798, there occurs the following line:
"Die Faulheit saugt uns mit ihre Vampyrenrüssel Mark und Blut ab" ("Laziness with its vampire snout sucks away our marrow and blood"). This may be compared with Jaromir's speech in Grillparzer's *Ahnfrau:*
Und die Angst mit Vampirrüssel
Saugt das Blut aus meinem Adern,
Aus dem Kopfe das Gehirn.
("And terror, with its vampire snout, sucks the blood from out my veins, the brain from out my head.")[36]

It is remarkable how exactly the literary language replicates the age-old superstitions concerning marrow and brain.

Tissot had argued that *all sexual activity is harmful,* by reason of the rush of blood to the brain, "starving the nerves, making them more susceptible to damage, and thereby inducing insanity." Solitary orgasm is the worst, making the victim liable to melancholy, fits, blindness, catalepsy, impotence, indigestion, idiocy, and paralysis. A French authority, Esquirol, commented in 1816 that masturbation "is recognized in all countries as a common cause of insanity" and also of suicide, melancholy, and epilepsy. German authorities added blindness and skin diseases. Sir William Ellis, superintendent of Hamwell Asylum, in 1852 listed hysteria, asthma, epilepsy, melancholia, mania, suicide, dementia, and general paralysis. In 1812, in the first American textbook on psychiatry, Benjamin Rush wrote that "the solitary vice" had worse consequences than "the morbid effects of intemperance with women," namely "seminal weakness, impotence, dysury, tabes dorsalis, pulmonary consumption, dimness of sight, vertigo, epilepsy, hypochondriasis, loss of memory, fatuity, and death." The whole nosology of known diseases was gradually being attributed to masturbation. Alarmed doctors suggested all manner of remedies. S. G. Vogel, in his *Unterricht für Eltern,* as early as 1785 recommended the placing of a silver wire through the boy's foreskin. Even adults commonly slept with the hand tied. J. L. Milton suggested a chastity belt. Spiked or toothed rings were made to fit round the penis. Yellowlees planned large-scale infibulation and "wiring all masturbators." John Moodie invented an intricate girdle of rubber with a steel grille and padlock, to prevent female masturbation.[37]

Although the arguments were in most cases traditional and imported, in the 1830s and 1840s American publicists and physicians began to repeat the injunctions of European writers with tireless enthusiasm, e.g., *The Secret Vice Exposed: Some Arguments Against Masturbation.* The inventor of Graham crackers wrote a widely read attack on masturbation and other excesses of sensuality in his *Lecture to Young Men* (1834).[38] Dr. William Acton's treatise on *The Functions and Disorders of the Reproductive Organs in Childhood, Youth, Adult Age and Advanced Life, Considered in their Physiological, Social, and Moral Relations* went through eight editions between 1857 and 1894. Regarding the tender youth, Acton writes warningly:

He does not know that to his immature frame every sexual indulgence is unmitigated evil. He does not think that to his inexperienced mind and heart every illicit pleasure is a degradation, to be bitterly regretted hereafter — a link in a chain that does not need many to be too strong to break. His Intellect has become sluggish and enfeebled, and if his evil habits are persisted in, he may end in becoming a drivelling idiot or a peevish valetudinarian. Such boys are to be seen in all stages of degeneration, but what we have described is but the result towards which *they all* are tending.[39]

Quoting from "a pamphlet lately printed by a clergyman" but "altering its phraseology a little, to adapt it to my book," Acton writes, "Many cases of the loss of reason end in imbecile and drivelling old age, as the inevitable result of the expenditure of the vital forces in sinful gratification" as is well known; and in a chapter on "Insanity Arising from Masturbation" he states flatly: "That insanity is a consequence of the habit, is now beyond a doubt," adding in a footnote, "especially with regard to the central portion of the cerebellum," which shows impressive scientific precision in locating the exact source of semen. Many pages later he still advised the aged, "Do not attempt to spend a great deal out of your small capital."[40] For his untiring and laudable efforts, Dr. Acton was ultimately knighted by Queen Victoria.

From the French of L. F. E. Bergeret was translated, in 1870, *The Preventive Obstacle, or Conjugal Onanism, The Dangers and Inconveniences to the Individual, to the Family, and to Society, of Frauds in the Accomplishment of the Generative Functions,* which used the popular term "onanism" with at least accuracy for coitus interruptus. Bergeret's book was primarily an attack on birth control, allegedly an especially American practice. Dio Lewis' *Chastity, or, Our Secret Sins* (1874) was often quoted, advocating limitation of sexuality even in marriage. N. F. Cooke's *Satan in Society, by a Physician* (1876) was a widely read attack on sexuality, quite influential because of the then great prestige of physicians. Joseph W. Howe's *Excessive Venery, Masturbation, and Continence: The Etiology, Pathology, and Treatment of the Diseases Resulting from Venereal Excesses, Masturbation, and Continence* (1887) was originally lectures to students in Medicine at New York University. J. H. Kellogg, *Plain Facts for Old and Young,* published in 1888 in Burlington, Iowa was suspicious not only of masturbation, prostitution, and abortion but also of "immoderate" indulgence even within marriage.[41] One of the most influential of all sexologies of the last century was the variously titled treatise of which the 1896 revision by Drs. Edward B. Foote, Sr. and Jr., was called *Plain Home Talk About the Human System.* It warned against becoming an

easy victim to a habit which taps the very fountains of nervo-vitality, and drains from the blood all its purest and most strengthening qualities. . . . In men this nervous loss is accompanied with an expenditure of some of the most vital fluids in the system — those secreted by the testicular glands, and which are composed of the most vital elements of the blood. In women, the nervous waste is simply accompanied with expenditure of glandular secretions of not much more vital value than the saliva or spittle of the mouth. [However, say the doctors authoritatively], there are men made up so strong in their sexual organs, having excessively large cerebellums or back heads, that can endure a great amount of sexual indulgence; these persons, in some instances, kill off a great many wives.[42]

Among this selection of books, A. J. Ingersoll's *In Health* (fourth edition, 1899) contained the extraordinary argument that such ills as hysteria were caused by denial of normal and necessary sexuality.[43]

Against the unmitigated evils and even fatal effects of masturbation, strenuous medical measures were obviously imperative. In 1820, a Dr. Weinhold of Halle advocated infibulation, a harmless operation he had successfully carried out on youthful onanists.

The operation itself is easy and almost entirely painless, as are the soldering and affixing of the metal seal. . . . The foreskin is drawn forward and gently compressed between a pair of perforated metal plates, so that when a hollow needle containing a core of lead wire is stuck through it, this is hardly felt. When the wire has been drawn through, it is bent, so that it cannot press on the adjacent parts; both the two ends are now brought together and soldered together with a small soldering-club. As soon as the knot, which is about the size of a lentil, has cooled off, a solid object is held against it; a small metal seal is pressed on it and this is afterwards kept in safety. This makes it quite impossible to open the infibulation and afterwards secretly close it again without the seal, without this being discovered at the next inspection.[44]

The value of the device also for birth control was evident. According to Dr. Weinhold, it could be left on for life on those who obviously could not achieve an economic position to maintain and provide for a family.

In America, John Humphrey Noyes, founder of the utopian Oneida community, and Dr. Alice Bunker Stockham, popular writer on matters concerning women's health, both made strong criticism of contemporary marital relationships. Noyes advocated *karezza* or *coitus reservatus*, imitating an old Hindu practice. Following his lead, Dr. Stockham advocated a form of birth control based on the ability of the male to enjoy intercourse without ejaculation. In this manner, women would avoid pregnancy; men, loss of manhood. What the practice might do to women's enjoyment was ignored, because of the strongly defended fiction that women had no such base feelings.[45]

In direct contradiction of this belief, however, young girls (despite the small damage to them of the practice) must be protected from the evils of masturbation. The remedy was simple and surgical: excision of the clitoris. Clitoridectomy was introduced in England about 1858 by Dr. Isaac Baker Brown, respected London surgeon, later president of the Medical Society of London.[46] The equivalent operation on boys, amputation of the penis, seemed impractical. Instead, in their zeal to extirpate masturbation, doctors in the late nineteenth century performed circumcision routinely on the newborn as a deterrent. The operation probably did more for parental anxiety, with its mixed motives, than it benefited its subjects. But nowhere is absolute power over other human beings more unquestioned than in parents. And parents, oddly, are no better than the ordinary run of people.

It is perhaps safe to say that circumcision has never deterred masturbation. Nor does contemporary scientific opinion support the surgical procedure. "The American Academy of Pediatricians concluded in 1971 and again in 1975: 'There is no absolute indication for routine circumcision of the newborn.'"[47] Pediatricians, however,

tend to be better informed psychiatrically than the obstetrical surgeons who perform the operation. Nor does scientific evidence
support the purpose of such surgery. The best-informed contemporary authorities state unequivocally. "There is no established medical
evidence that masturbation regardless of frequency leads to mental
illness."[48] In fact, coitus itself occasions no "loss of manhood." Ex-
perimental measurements showed that "strength and endurance of
the... muscles are apparently not adversely affected early in the day
following nocturnal coitus."[49]

It is not difficult, however, to find colloquial evidence for the
persistence of old beliefs. Some random samples — from a call girl:
"Every time you have an orgasm it takes a fluid that is drawn from
the base of the spine. The loss of that fluid drains off energy and
slows up your brain and makes you physically tired;"[50] — from a
psychiatrist: "At recess between two periods one of my schoolmates
said to me: 'If you go on masturbating like this any longer, you will
go crazy.'[51] Many people... even now believe that the secretion
comes from the spine, that the spinal marrow is dried up by this
famous 'self-abuse,' and that finally the brain dries up too, and so
people become feeble-minded;"[52] — from a psychoanalyst (quoting
a German-speaking patient): "My father believes to this day that
masturbation causes the spinal cord to run out;"[53] and (quoting a
phobic patient): "The patient had also been repeatedly told by his
parents that if he masturbated his spinal cord would leak out — the
implication being that the ejaculated semen was part of the spinal
cord."[54]

The routine study of anatomy among medical students has destroyed the notion that the brain, even especially the cerebellum, is
the source of semen. Nonetheless, there has been a certain lag in
exorcising other old superstitions about sexuality: "Half of the medical students graduating from five Philadelphia medical schools in
1959 still thought that masturbation was a frequent cause of mental
illness. Worse yet, a fifth of the medical school faculty members

shared the same misconception."[55] This remains a commentary on the inadequate training of physicians in modern psychiatry.

An Edwardian-bred generation no doubt has sound oedipal franchise for revolt against parental repression. But on the lips of their great-grandchildren, with most such battles more than won, "Victorian" is a tiresome cliché. The Victorians did not invent anxiety about sexualilty — though, progressive in all things, Victorians did exacerbate acutely the terrors of preceding centuries.[56] And they suffered, as much as any, from ignorance of the forgotten past.

Freud early took a conservative position on masturbation. He thought it might lead to "organic injury [through] some unknown mechanism," though there is little enough medical evidence for his fear. But, more importantly, Freud thought that masturbation can lead to a "fixation of infantile sexual aims and a persistence of psychic infantilism which predisposes to the occurrence of neurosis."[57] Freud wrote that masturbation

vitiates the character through indulgence, and this in more than one way. In the first place, it teaches people to achieve important aims without taking trouble and by easy paths instead of through an energetic exertion of force — that is, it follows the principle that *sexuality lays down the pattern* of behavior; secondly, in the phantasies that accompany satisfaction the sexual object is raised to a degree of excellence which is not easily found again in reality.[58]

Inasmuch as all societies require control of sexuality, perhaps repression is the price we pay for civilization.[59] At the same time, masturbation is needed to establish the primacy of genital over pregenital libido, fixation at which earlier psychosexual stages is conspicuous in neurosis and psychosis. Thus, like the transitional stage of admiration and emulation of one's own sex, it is evidently one stage of normal maturation.

In 1926, Freud modified his views "concerning masturbation as a cause of neurotic disturbances and actually proposed that at times it was a protection against such disturbances. But he still recommended a moderate degree of suppression of masturbation on the basis of certain cultural implications."[60] In some severely repressed neurotic patients, the return of infantile masturbation might represent a regression in the service of the ego. "This probably provides a powerful protection against the subsequent development of neurosis in the individual. But does it not at the same time involve an extraordinary loss of the aptitude for cultural achievements? There is a good deal to suggest that here we are faced by a new Scylla and Charybdis."[61] Freud would argue that, as in all forms of pleasure whether genital or pregenital, the conscious mind should remain sovereign. Understanding often means encountering unpleasant subjects, and freedom lies in sometimes-painful knowledge of the past, individual and collective, psychological and culture-historical.

Ignorance of the world, of ourselves, and of the past gives immortality to error. Nor is this all. Erroneous beliefs are not without their unpredictable and undesirable consequences. Behaviors based on wrong conclusions are not transformed, in some random or magical way, into beneficial results simply because the beliefs themselves persist. False beliefs have the same price, adaptively, as any other random mutation has biologically. The colorful Stone Age belief that semen originates in the head has not really benefited mankind, being implicated instead in nobly meant but questionably useful headhunting (even when sanctioned by religion), false ideas and bizarre sexual practices concerning puberty, gross superstitions about the facts of life, and centuries of incalculable anxiety.

Summary

The intercontinental distribution of a group of beliefs, not necessarily connected logically, and not necessarily correct, indicates the persistence of ideational elements of Old Stone Age thinking into modern times. The occurrence of the complex in both aboriginal Americas indicates not independent discoveries of objective physiological fact but only the Mesolithic cultural horizons of the first human inhabitants of the New World. In the Old World also, there are relicts of a bone cult of the first hunters, and even evidence of head collecting by pre-*sapiens* Neanderthaloids in Europe and Asia. Given local emphasis of various elements, the complex of ideas includes the following. Bones are given by the male parent, and bones can magically reconstitute the whole animal. As the main storehouse of bone marrow, the brain is the source of semen, via the spinal cord. The supply is limited. The fertility of the head is assimilated to cosmic fertility of the sun, rain, lightning. Fire, light, lightning, and seed are all aspects of the same holy male mystery. The fertility of humans, wild animals, and fields can be increased by collecting severed human heads. Fat-marrow and bones are appropriate sacrifice to the immortal spirits, the eternal gods. Immortality also consists in the "continence" of muelos-seed, achieved in various ways. Adult manhood is not the result of endogenous forces but must be obtained from outside through a variety of methods, including homosexual acts. Virility is secreted with the semen, in all ejaculation of whatever kind; virility can thus on occasion be made a gift. Loss of manhood, power, and ultimately life itself results from the "spending" of the life-force, which is a finite capital.

Although these beliefs have been held through many hundred millennia over most of the world, not one or any combination of them is correct.

In the infantile encounter with persons and things, the individual, often under emotional duress, makes serious misconstruals of reality that have an alarmingly long life, in adult neurosis or psychosis. The "permanence of experience" perhaps has a neurological substrate. But to the *neurosis* and the *psychosis* as ways of misrepresenting current reality in the processing of new experience, we must now add the *archosis*. An "archosis" is a massive and fundamental misapprehension of reality, often of incalculable antiquity culturally, yet which has been inherited from human predecessors, in the normal fashion of any cultural bequest. Some archoses, such as the belief that semen is held in the head, may be even older than our immediate hominid species, trailing back through Neanderthaloid *pekinensis* even to brain-eating Australopithecine *erectus*.

Another archosis, belief in the separable soul — "that unhappy word has been the refuge of empty minds ever since the world began!" — is arguably as old as Neanderthal burials and the Neanderthal-inhabited caves.[62] We may even occasionally witness the birth of a new archosis, as in the well-documented case of Bekker's "onanism" in producing insanity — to be sure with its antecedents in classic thought and in old European muelos-fantasies.

A frightening proportion of all culture is arguably archosis, more especially sacred culture. In another place I have suggested the reasons that religions, born in crisis cults, are so commonly unrealistic ghost-dance responses to unresolved problems, though they pretend to be final solutions and are fanatically defended against alternative hypotheses. This aspect of culture is so patently group-hallucinosis, based on now obsolescent fantasy, that the critical individual, commonly in adolescence, is able to tear away the mildewed holy veil of oedipal symbols — and to substitute his own, if he needs to flee the anguish of remembered childhood realities. How much of dreamwork is the necessary sorting out of old social and personal memories?

We are arrogant apes staggering from crisis to catastrophe. We toast a friend with the *skoal* of a beheaded enemy; the enemy *host* is the same *Host* that we eat in sacred ceremony. Military machismo still dimly confuses weapon with phallus, like the hunter in a Paleolithic African rockpainting, confuses all shooting with orgasm, and killing with essential manhood. Men thought, as early as the Old Stone Age, that they knew the facts of life and built their most sacred, grotesque, deluded cults upon them.

If Culture is our ecological adaptation, then diverse cultures are the biological speciations, the random mutations by which we live or die (in our Wilderness what Moses will discover our Snake of immortality?). We play the survival game with confidence since we know in pious certainty that a cosmic Papa will return our marbles when we lose. Extinction is not for keeps. We rush into death because we know we do not die.

Notes

1. Hellenistic antisexuality, in which St. Paul is deeply immersed, is itself an aspect of the pervading "crisis cult" of Platonism. W. La Barre, *The Ghost Dance*, (Chicago: University of Chicago Press, 1970), pp. 494–500. Plato's political "noble lie" parallels Christianity's Orphic noble lie of immortality (pp. 526–27).

2. Salomon Reinach, *Orpheus: A General History of Religions* (London: William Heinemann, 1909), p. 285. St. Simeon, in *Patrologia Graeca*, 52:1464, in J. Hastings, ed., *Encyclopedia of Religion and Ethics (Hastings Encyclopedia)*, 13 vols. (New York: Scribner's 1908–1926), 8:789. Traditional religion in China was inimical to Buddhist monasticism, since the latter was counter to the Chinese familial organization of society: "In A.D. 714 a fierce persecution broke out, during which 12,000 religious of both sexes were compelled to return to the secular state, while in a still more bitter persecution in the following century 4600 religious houses were closed and 200,000 monks and nuns were secularized" *Hastings Encyclopedia*, 10:293–94. Taoism also felt the hand of the state, since its priests had also been celibate since the first Sung emperor.

3. Origen: Eusebius Pamphilus, *Ecclesiasticae Historiae*, vi, 8; 2 vols. (Cambridge: At the University Press, 1720); Justin, *Apologia pro Christianis*, xix, in J. P. Migne, *Patrologia Cursus Completus*, 102 vols. (Seria Graeca, 1856–1866), vi, col. 373.

4. Roman law: Suetonius, *Domitian,* vii, On Christianity as the neurosis of St. Paul, La Barre, *Ghost Dance*, pp. 603–10.

5. *Hastings Encyclopedia*, "Celibacy," 3:272. Jovinian: G. Rattray Taylor, *Sex in History* (New York: Vanguard Press, 1954), p. 52.

6. Taylor, *Sex in History*, pp. 51–52.

7. Taylor, *Sex in History*, p. 86. With the medieval penchant for finding meaning where we see only the accidental, it was said that the Church of *Roma* had reversed the teaching of the Church of *Amor*, much as it preached of love (p. 101).

8. Taylor, *Sex in History,* pp. 54 – 56, citing G. May, *Social Control of Sexual Expression* (London: Allen & Unwin, 1930). At one time, marriages were legal only when made during a specified twenty-five weeks of the year, between 8:00 A.M. and noon. Abolished in the Reformation, the regulation was restored by Laud and made statute law in the reign of George II, infractions being punishable by fourteen years penal servitude. J. C. Jeaffreson, *Brides and Bridals* (London: Hurst & Blackett, 1872), in Taylor, *Sex in History,* p. 64.

9. Taylor, *Sex in History,* p. 56, quoting W. H. Lecky, *The History of the Rise and Influence of the Spirit of Rationalism in Europe* (London: Longmans, Green 1880).

10. Plato, *Republic,* 414, bc.

11. Eric Partridge, *Shakespeare's Bawdy: A Literary and Psychological Essay and a Comprehensive Glossary* (London: Routledge, 1947), p. 144. Shakespeare appears to refer to masturbation in his Sonnets, especially Sonnet 4; 6.5, "forbidden usury"; 6.6 (the notion that seminal emission diminishes the life span; cf. 11.3 and 129.1); 6.13, and 9.14. Stephen Booth, ed., *Shakespeare's Sonnets* (New Haven and London: Yale University Press, 1977).

12. Partridge, *Shakespeare's Bawdy,* pp. 153 – 54.

13. Partridge, *Shakespeare's Bawdy,* pp. 165 – 66.

14. Richard Burton, *The Book of a Thousand Nights and a Night,* 10 vols., (Benares, India: Kamashastra Society, 1885 – 1888), quoted in Byron Farwell, *Burton: A Biography of Sir Richard Francis Burton* (London: Longmans, Green, 1963), p. 372.

15. *Oxford English Dictionary,* s.v. "spermaceti."

16. *Oxford English Dictionary,* s.v. "sperm."

17. G. B. Goode et al., *Natural History of Useful Aquatic Animals,* in *The Fisheries and Fishing Industries of the United States,* 7 vols. (Washington, D.C.: Government Printing Office, 1884), sec. 1, p. 6. Among whalemen the spout is deemed poisonous, corrosive, and even blinding (H. Melville, *Moby Dick,* ch. 85, "The Fountain"). In his novel of 1851, Melville seems to have regarded brains as an aphrodisiac, in reporting of "young bucks... continually dining upon calves brains" (ch. 65, "The Whale as a Dish"); compare the "young whales, in the highest health, and swelling with noble aspirations... in the warm flush and May of life, with all their panting lard about them" (ch. 71, "The Pequod Meets the Virgin"). Melville also reports a whalemen's superstition, "that strange spectacle observable in all sperm Whales dying — the turning sunwards of the head" (ch. 116, "The Dying

Whale"). Another passage suggests the traditional belief in brain – sperm equivalence: "So like a choice casket is it secreted in him that I have known some whalemen who peremptorily deny that the Sperm Whale has any other brain than that palpable semblance of one formed by the cubic yards of his sperm magazine" (ch. 80, "The Nut").

18. Richard McCurdy, ed., *The Notebooks of Leonardo da Vinci* (New York: Braziller, 1954), p. 24.

19. Herbert Wendt, *The Sex Life of the Animals* (New York: Simon & Schuster, 1965), p. 52

20. McCurdy, *Notebooks*, p. 161.

21. McCurdy, *Notebooks*, p. 128.

22. B. Farrell, in Morris Philipson, ed., *Leonardo da Vinci: Aspects of the Renaissance Genius* (New York: Braziller, 1966), p. 245.

23. K. R. Eissler, "Psychoanalytic Notes," in Philipson, *Leonardo*, p. 289.

24. Leonardo, *Quaderni d'Anatomia*, III, 3v, "Coition Figures and Other Studies," Windsor Castle, Royal Library, No. 19097 v, in Philipson, *Leonardo*, fig. 70. The female equivalent of the Leonardo duct is described in Pliny, *Natural History*, XL, lxvii, 178, which appears to equate milk with semen.

25. Martial, *Epigrams*, II, xliii, 13 – 14 and XI, lxiii, 3 – 4; English translation by Walter C. A. Ker, 2 vols. (New York: Putnam, 1925 – 1927), 1:235, 2:290. Jeffrey Henderson has materials on classic Greek attitudes toward masturbation. *The Maculate Muse: Obscene Language in the Attic Comedy* (New Haven: Yale University Press, 1975).

26. The nonmention of masturbation in Loyola's *Spiritual Exercises* is regarded by Spitz as "a proof that its direct suppression was of little concern to the Catholic Church in the seventeenth century." René A. Spitz, "Authority and Masturbation: Some Remarks on a Bibliographical Investigation," in Irwin M. Marcus and John J. Francis, eds., *Masturbation from Infancy to Senescence*, pp. 381 – 409 (New York: International University Press, 1975), p. 385 n. 2. (But Loyola was sixteenth century.)

27. Story of Onan: *Genesis* 38:9; cf. *Leviticus* 15:16 – 17. Robert Burton, *The Anatomy of Melancholy*, I, iii, II, iv; also III, ii, VI, v. (1651 ed., pp. 205, 581).

28. S. A. Tissot, *Dissertation sur les maladies produites par la masturbation*, 3d ed., Lausanne: Chapins, 1770), p. 8, cited by Spitz, "Authority," p. 386.

29. Jean-Philippe Dutoit-Mambrini, *De l'onanie: ou discours philosophique et moral sur la luxure artificielle, et sur les crimes relatifs* (Lausanne: F. Grasser, 1760) chs. 7 – 9, cited in Herbert Moller, "Wet Dreams and the

Ejaculate," *Maledicta* (1980), 4(2):249 – 51, p. 250. A. Hume, *Onanism; or a Treatise upon Disorders Produced by Masturbation* (1755).

30. Duns Scotus, in Alex Comfort, *The Anxiety Makers: Some Curious Preoccupations of the Medical Profession* (New York: Thomas Nelson, 1963), ch. 3, "The Rise and Fall of Self-Abuse," p. 70. Francis Bacon noted that the ancient authorities believed "much use of Venus doth dim the eyesight" (Edward Gifford, "The Evil Eye in Medical History," *American Journal of Ophthalmology* [1958], 44:237 – 43. In his "History of Life and Death, with Observation Naturall and Experimentall for the Prolonging of Life," (*Essays*, London: Logographic Press, 1787), 2:353 – 480, Bacon writes that "the head is the principal feat of all the fpirits, being great wafters of the body" (p. 383); gold in medicines prolongs life (p. 418); "abftinence from fenfual pleafures, abate and diminish the fpirits, which being reduced to a quantity fufficient to maintain life, do make leffer wafte on the body" (p. 437); and "the fpirits are wafted by. . . intemperate and unfeafonable venery" (p. 442).

31. Voltaire, *Dictionnaire philosophique*, s.v. "Onanisme," quoted in Comfort, *Anxiety Makers*, p. 75.

32. Ferreres, *Compendium Theologicae Moralis* (1925), quoted in Comfort, *Anxiety Makers*, p. 71.

33. Jean-Pierre David, *Traité de la Nutrition et de l'accroisement précédé d'un dissertation sur l'usage des eaux de l'amnios* (1771), quoted in Gaston Bachelard, *The Psychoanalysis of Fire* (Boston: Beacon Press, 1968), p. 47.

34. G. L. Simons, *Sex and Superstition* (New York: Barnes & Noble, 1973), p. 150.

35. François Lallemand, *Des pertes séminales involuntaires*, 3 vols. (Paris: Bechet, 1836 – 1843). See also collection of medical opinions in *Lancet*, (1843 – 1844) 1:46 – 53, 210 – 16, 328 – 29, 398 – 403, 478 – 81; John S. Haller, Jr., and Robin M. Haller, *The Physician and Sexuality in Victorian America* (Urbana: University of Illinois Press, 1974), 2:211 – 25.

36. Ernest Jones, *On the Nightmare* (New York: Liveright, 1971), p. 120.

37. All references in this paragraph are from Simons, *Sex and Superstition*, pp. 151 – 53.

38. *The Secret Vice Exposed: Some Arguments Against Masturbation* (New York: Arno Press, 1974); Sylvester Graham, *A Lecture to Young Men*, 3d ed. (Boston: C. W. Light, 1837).

39. Sir William Acton, *The Functions and Disorders of the Reproductive Organs in Childhood, Youth, Adult Age and Advanced Life, Considered in Their Physiological, Social, and Moral Relations* (Philadelphia: Blakiston,

1857), quoted in S. Marcus, *The Other Victorians: A Study of Sexuality and Pornography in Mid–Nineteenth-Century England* (New York: Basic Books, 1966), pp. 18–19.

40. Acton, *Functions and Disorders*, p. 313.

41. L. F. E. Bergeret, *The Preventive Obstacle, or Conjugal Onanism, the Dangers and Inconveniences to the Individual, to the Family, and to Society, of Frauds in the Accomplishment of the Generative Functions* (New York: Turner & Mignard, 1870); Dio Lewis, *Chastity, Or, Our Secret Sins* (Philadelphia and New York: G. Maclean, 1874); Nicholas Francis Cooke, *Satan in Society, By a Physician* (Cincinnati: C. F. Vent, 1876); Joseph W. Howe, *Excessive Venery, Masturbation, and Continence: The Etiology, Pathology and Treatment of the Diseases Resulting from Venereal Excesses, Masturbation, and Continence* (New York: Bermingham, 1887); and J. H. Kellogg, *Plain Facts for Old and Young* (Burlington, Iowa: Segner, 1884). All the above books have been reprinted by the Arno Press, New York, in 1974.

42. Edward B. Foote, Sr. and Jr., *Plain Home Talk About the Human System* (Chicago: Thompson & Thomas, 1896), pp. 137, 479–80, 872. The Footes, Sr. and Jr., appear to have invented the ingenious argument that pubic hair insulates the static electricity allegedly generated in the relation of the sexes (p. 630).

43. A. J. Ingersoll, *In Health*, 4th ed. (Boston: Lee and Shepherd, 1899).

44. Richard Lewinsohn, *A History of Sexual Customs* (New York: Longmans, Green, 1958), pp. 323–24, quoting Carl August Weinhold, *Von der Übervölkerung in Mittel-europa und deren Folgen auf die Staaten und ihre Civilization* (Halle, Germany: E. Anton, 1827), pp. 32ff.

45. A. C. Kinsey, et al., *Sexual Behavior in the Human Female* (Philadelphia: Saunders, 1953), p. 625; *Sexual Indulgence and Denial: Variations on Continence* (New York: Arno Press, 1974). Compare similar rationalizations in *masturbatio interrupta*. Karl Abraham, "Hysterical Dream States," pp. 90–124 in *Selected Papers* (London: Hogarth Press, 1927), p. 99.

46. Spitz, "Authority," p. 390. The article by Spitz contains an excellent bibliography, pp. 399–409. It appeared originally in the *Yearbook of Psychoanalysis* (1953), 9:113–45.

47. *Time*, August 31, 1981. For theories concerning the purposes of circumcision, see Vincent Crapanzano, "Rites of Return: Circumcision in Morocco," in Werner Muensterberger and L. Bryce Boyer, eds., *The Psychoanalytic Study of Society*, pp. 15–36, (New York: Psychohistory Press, 1980), pp. 20ff; La Barre, *Ghost Dance*, pp. 594–95 n. 12; La Barre,

They Shall Take Up Serpents: Psychology of the Southern Snakehandling Cult (Minneapolis: University of Minnesota Press, 1962), pp. 67 – 74; R. A. Graber, "A Psycho-Cultural Theory of Male Genital Mutilation," *Journal of Psychoanalytic Anthropology* (Fall 1981), 4(4):413 – 34. "By the 1950s the great majority of baby boys, from rich and poor families alike, were routinely circumcised in hospitals. One study of the records of 18 hospitals across the nation revealed that 83 percent of the 14,116 male infants born in 1973 had been circumcised. Among the births financed by a California medical program during the first quarter of 1976, 87 percent of the males were circumcised. [The only other country in the world that reports nearly so high a percentage is Australia, where the custom is on the way out, except for Semitic countries with the ritual requirement.] In England circumcision is virtually absent. In 1972... less than 1 percent of 400,000 boys under one year had the operation (0.41 percent). The Scandinavian countries never accepted circumcision, and most of Europe has abandoned it." Karen Erickson Paige, "The Ritual of Circumcision," *Human Nature* (May 1978), 1(5):43. See also R. P. Neuman, "Masturbation, Madness and the Modern Concepts of Childhood and Adolescence," *Journal of Social History,* Spring 1976, pp. 1 – 27; E. N. Preston, "Whither the Foreskin?," *Journal of the American Medical Association,* vol. 213, no. 11. According to studies cited by Paige, circumcision does not reduce the incidence of cancer of the cervix in the wives of circumcised men.

48. W. H. Masters and V. E. Johnson, *Human Sexual Response* (Boston: Little, Brown, 1966), quoted by John J. Francis and Irwin M. Marcus, "Masturbation — A Developmental View," in Irwin M. Marcus and John J. Francis, eds., *Masturbation from Infancy to Senescence* (pp. 9 – 51 (New York: International Universities Press, 1975), p. 37.

49. Warren R. Johnson, "Muscular Performance Following Coitus," *Journal of Sex Research* (August 1968), 4(3):247 – 48, p. 248.

50. Harold Greenwald, *The Call Girl: A Social and Psychoanalytic Study* (New York: Ballantine Books, 1958), p. 118.

51. Georg Groddeck, *Book of the Id* (New York: Vintage, 1961), p. 187.

52. Groddeck, *Book of the Id,* p. 43. When a boy, a distinguished psychologist "was about petrified lest I be losing my brain," and had a phobic displacement upward to his nose. G. Stanley Hall, *Life and Confessions of a Psychologist,* (New York: Appleton-Century-Crofts, 1923), pp. 131 – 33, quoted in Norman Kiell, *The Universal Experience of Adolescence* (New York: International Universities Press, 1964), pp. 184 – 85.

53. George Devereux, "Interpretation and Catheterization: The Fantasy of the Vaginalized Uretha," *Bulletin of the Menninger Clinic,* (1979), 43(6):545.

54. George Devereux, "Weeping, Urination and Grand Mal," *Journal of the Hillside Hospital* (January – April 1965), 14(1 – 2):101. Compare Hippocrates, *De Morbis,* "The sickness has its origin in the marrow of the backbone," with Lawrence Durrell, *The Black Book* (New York: Dutton, 1960), "My penis swells, turns purple, and my brains drop out of it" (p. 131). In an autobiography, an angry woman told her errant husband "he could throw his rubbish where his love went; and his tallow could go in the same place as his beer." Jeremy Seabrook, *Mother and Son* (New York: Pantheon Books, 1980), p. 163. In a contemporary novel, a boy thought masturbation would make his penis "grow as long and as thin as a shoelace" and that semen "was the cream of the brain power." John Cheever, *Falconer* (New York: Knopf, 1977), p. 119. Sometimes the fantasy is merely metaphorical: "The snail trailing a moist streak after it as it crawls [is] so using up its vitality." Louis Ginsberg, *Legends of the Jews,* (New York: Simon and Schuster, 1961), p. 23.

55. H. I. Lief, "Teaching Doctors about Sex," in R. and E. Brecher, eds., *An Analysis of Human Sexual Response* (Boston: Little, Brown, 1966), p. 415 *n. 3.*

56. A distinguished Yale historian arrives at the same conclusion. Peter Gay, "Victorian Sexuality: Old Texts and New Insights," *American Scholar,* (1980), 49: 372–78, contains a valuable bibliography pp. 376–78. Compare J. S. Haller and R. M. Haller, *The Physician and Sexuality in Victorian America* Urbana: University of Illinois Press, 1974.

57. Sigmund Freud, "Contribution to a Discussion of Masturbation [1912]," *Standard Edition* (London: Hogarth Press, 1959), quoted in Sidney Levin, "The Relation of Various Affects to Masturbation Conflicts," pp. 305 – 13 in Marcus and Francis, *Masturbation,* pp. 307 – 8.

58. Sigmund Freud, "'Civilized' sexual ethics and modern nervous sickness [1908]," in *Standard Edition,* 9:199 – 200. Freud is almost certainly wrong in confining repression and suppression only to 'civilized' peoples, but his generalization may safely be extended to all.

59. Sigmund Freud, *Civilization and Its Discontents* (London: Hogarth Press, 1930).

60. Levin, "Masturbation Conflicts," p. 308.

61. Freud, quoted by Levin, "Masturbation Conflicts," pp. 308–9. Unconsidered easy and often psychiatrically naive libertarian views are found in

M. F. DeMartino, ed., *Human Autoerotic Practices* (New York: Human Sciences Press, 1979).
   62. Norman Douglas, *South Wind*, ch. 11. I owe the term "archosis" to Caspar Schmidt, M.D. from his reading of *The Ghost Dance* (private conversation).

Postscript

The Vienna Psychoanalytic Society held discussions a generation ago that may be regarded as definitive; see Herman Nunberg and Ernst Federn, eds., *Minutes of the Vienna Psychoanalytic Society 1908–1918* (New York: International Universities Press, 1973), with the "Group Discussion on Masturbation" beginning in part 3 (1910–1911). Eduard Hitschmann noted (3:336) that the masturbator spares himself from the struggle for the love-object, which is a model for the rest of life's struggles; also, by serving as an early target for reproaches having to do with sexuality—often complicated by and imposing trauma of prohibition—it may become the root for many an obsessional idea. Paul Federn (3:377) wondered how far masturbation has a harmful effect on the basis of its being regarded as sinful, and to what extent it is harmful per se.

   Viktor Tausk (3:341–45) noted that whenever the subject feels inadequate in a situation he returns to masturbation. He has a hypersensitivity to imperfections in an object, having been spoiled by fantasy. As a result of seeing in a woman nothing but a genital, he loses any relationship to the totality of woman; therefore, soon after gratification, alienation from the object sets in, and synthesis of the perverse component into normal love fails to take place, leading to devaluation of women, with a special relationship between masturbation and cynicism. The masturbator is convinced that in consequence of his impaired potency, women must despise him, and then he considers them insatiable; therein both an overestimation and an underestimation of women ensues. Is a hypercathexis of sexuality the reason for the masturbator's inability to concentrate? Further, he is almost never satisfied because he is always expecting salvation. Masturbation ruins love life insofar as it reduces the capacity for lovemaking and hence drives men to prostitutes. Freud (3:358–59) defended Tausk, since many analysts also think the central problem in "choice of neurosis" does in fact lie in the question of masturbation.

Otto Rank (3:358–59) noted displacement of the defensive struggle against masturbation onto oral, eating, and speaking disturbances; exaggerated punctuality and obsessional setting of dates are typical of the struggle. Theodor Reik (3:362) noted the asocial nature of masturbation and neurosis alike: that the subject hides it, cuts off communication. The discussion was continued in part 4 (1912–1918). Osa Molchfass pointed out that masturbation is, in a sense, intrinsically homosexual: it is easier to transfer from self-sex to same-sex than to other-sex libido. In an "Epilog to the Discussions" (4:92–96) Freud states (4:93):

A priori, one is forced to oppose the assertion that masturbation has to be harmless; on the contrary, there must be cases in which masturbation is harmful. Since the etiology of the neuroses is given by way of the conflict between infantile sexuality and the opposition of the ego (repression), masturbation, which is only an executive of infantile sexuality, cannot a priori be presented as harmless. The question of when masturbation is harmful and when it is not cannot be answered in general terms.

This is the irony: Old Stone Age men thought they knew all about loss of manhood, yet our most subtle and profound modern authority considers the question unresolved, moot.